Mary Cassatt

To Lee, with much love,
Nancy Plain

Mary Cassatt

An Artist's Life

Nancy Plain

A People in Focus Book

DILLON PRESS
New York

Maxwell Macmillan Canada
Toronto

Maxwell Macmillan International
New York   Oxford   Singapore   Sydney

To my mother and to the memory of my father

Acknowledgments
The author would like to thank her inspiring editor, Joyce Stanton, for making this book possible. Many thanks also to Zehavah Goldberg, of the Graduate Center of the City University of New York, for her expert reading of the manuscript.

Photo Credits
Front and back jacket covers courtesy of The Metropolitan Museum of Art (front: *Self-Portrait*, 1878; back: *Young Mother Sewing*, 1902)

The Historical Society of Pennsylvania: 14; The Pennsylvania Academy of the Fine Arts: 24, 39; Musée d'Orsay: 31; Nelson-Atkins Museum of Art: 47; Maxwell Galeries: 48; Musée Marmottan: 54; The Metropolitan Museum of Art: 87; Bryn Mawr College Library: 106; The Chicago Historical Society: 110-111; National Gallery of Art: 114; Smithsonian Institution: 115, 134, 140, 144.

Book design by Carol Matsuyama

Library of Congress Cataloging-in-Publication Data
Plain, Nancy.
    Mary Cassatt, An artist's life / by Nancy Plain. — 1st ed.
       p. cm. — (People in focus)
    Includes bibliographical references and index.
    ISBN 0-87518-597-5 HC   ISBN 0-382-24720-5 PBK
      1. Cassatt, Mary, 1844–1926—Juvenile literature. 2. Painters—United States—Biography—Juvenile literature. [1. Cassatt, Mary, 1844–1926. 2. Artists. 3. Women—Biography.] I. Title. II. Series.
ND237.C3P58 1994
759.13—dc20   93-46578
[B]

Describes the life of Mary Cassatt, America's most famous woman painter, and her association with the French Impressionist movement.

Copyright © 1994 by Nancy Plain

All rights reserved. No part of this book may be reproduced or transmitted in any form or by any means, electronic or mechanical, including photocopying, recording, or by any information storage and retrieval system, without permission in writing from the Publisher.

Dillon Press   Maxwell Macmillan Canada, Inc.
Macmillan Publishing Company   1200 Eglinton Avenue East
866 Third Avenue   Suite 200
New York, NY 10022   Don Mills, Ontario M3C 3N1

Macmillan Publishing Company is part of the Maxwell Communication Group of Companies.

First edition

Printed in the United States of America

10 9 8 7 6 5 4 3 2 1

Contents

Introduction	6
Chapter One — Paris and Pennsylvania	8
Chapter Two — "A Passion for Line and Color"	16
Chapter Three — Finding the Way	26
Chapter Four — Old Masters and a New Art	34
Chapter Five — "There Is Someone Who Feels as I Do"	49
Chapter Six — Mary Cassatt, Impressionist	63
Chapter Seven — Family Cares	80
Chapter Eight — Japanese Prints and a Chicago Mural	99
Chapter Nine — "I Am American"	122
Chapter Ten — War and Roses	145
Appendix One — Mary Cassatt: A Time Line	155
Appendix Two — Sources	158
Selected Bibliography	165
Index	167

Introduction

"I am not willing to admit that a woman can draw that well," said the brilliant French painter Edgar Degas. He was stingy with his praise, but he spoke his mind as he admired the pictures in a Paris art gallery.

The woman who could draw that well was Degas's good friend—the American artist Mary Cassatt. The occasion was her first one-woman show, and at forty-six, she was at the height of her creative powers. At a time when few women even considered having careers, Cassatt had achieved fame as an artist. Many of France's finest painters now came to her exhibit to marvel at the originality and fresh beauty of her work.

Mary Cassatt was the only American to join the French Impressionist movement. Degas, Monet, Renoir, Pissarro, Morisot—these were Cassatt's fellow revolutionaries. They changed forever the way people look at art. Often painting mothers and children, Cassatt gave the world pictures that celebrate color and light and everyday life. Her oils, pastels, and color prints are treasured today in museums and private collections throughout the world. Success, however, did not come overnight.

When Mary was only sixteen, she knew that she wanted to be a professional artist. Her well-to-do parents were amazed. In the 1860s, proper young ladies were expected to devote themselves to a husband and children. Their days would be filled with family and household cares. In the Cassatts' world, art was suitable for a hobby—not a career.

The predictable woman's place was not what Mary wanted. Her unusual ambition to become a "real" artist worried her father so much that he blurted out, "I would almost rather see you dead!" But Mary had determination in her bright gray eyes and daring in her soul. She held fast to her dream. At the same time, she was always practical about making it come true.

The dream sustained Mary through hard years of study, and it led her to Paris. There she found herself "at home" with the independent-minded Impressionists. And she never stopped painting. This is the story of a woman, born in a small town in Pennsylvania, who traveled a long road to become one of the world's great artists.

Chapter One

Paris and Pennsylvania

Mary Stevenson Cassatt was born just before midnight on May 22, 1844, in Allegheny City, Pennsylvania. Although the town has since been swallowed up by the city of Pittsburgh, Allegheny City was then a quiet little settlement on the banks of the Ohio River. Mary's father, Robert Cassatt, had built a comfortable house on a hill overlooking the river, and this was her first home.

Her mother, Katherine, called her new baby May. Mary's father called his daughter Mame. Whatever the nickname, a loving, close-knit family welcomed Mary Cassatt. Her older sister and brothers were Lydia, Alexander (Aleck), and Robert (Robbie). Mary's younger brother, Joseph Gardner (Gard), would be born in 1849.

The generations that had come before gave the Cassatts a strong sense of their own identity. Robert

Cassatt could trace his ancestry back to one Jacques Cossart, a French Huguenot (Protestant) who moved to Holland in the 1600s to escape religious persecution. Cossart's son married a Dutch woman, and the young couple was brave enough to cross the Atlantic Ocean to settle in New Amsterdam (New York) in 1662. In America, the family's heritage was expanded to include Scots-Irish, and in the 1700s, the name Cossart was changed to Cassat. In the 1840s, Mary's father added the final "t" to the family name.

One of Katherine Cassatt's ancestors, Alexander Johnston, had sailed from Ireland to America, where he served as an attorney for George Washington. Katherine also liked to recount the adventures of her grandfather Colonel James Johnston. This old soldier had fought in the American Revolution and lived with the Cassatts until he died, two years before Mary was born.

Thus the family was deeply rooted in the American past, and the Cassatt children grew up hearing stories about the early years of the nation. Mary's parents were proud of their status as an "old American family."

American history was only part of the Cassatt children's education. Their mother had great intellectual curiosity and was interested in many aspects of culture. Katherine Cassatt encouraged her children to read and to appreciate art and music. French civilization was her special love. As a young girl in Pittsburgh, she had studied with a woman who had been educated in Paris. As a result, Katherine spoke perfect French by the age of twelve. Now she arranged French lessons for her children, too. (Fluent French came in handy for Mary later on, although she never got rid of her Pennsylvania accent!)

Katherine Cassatt was the strong, steady anchor of her family. She was highly intelligent and organized family life with a firm hand. Yet she was gentle, calm, and kind. Katherine taught her children her highest values—loyalty to family and personal responsibility.

Mary and her mother were intensely devoted to each other all their lives. Mrs. Cassatt was the family member who would best understand Mary's desire to paint. And it was from her mother that Mary acquired her lifelong sense of determination and perseverance.

The personalities of Mary and her father sometimes clashed. While her mother was always dependable, Mr. Cassatt could be irritable and stubborn. And from his point of view, Mame could be "dreadfully headstrong." But the Cassatt stubbornness also helped father and daughter weather their differences and meet on the common ground of family love. They always remained involved in each other's lives. In fact, a sister-in-law would one day observe of Mary, "The only being she seems to think of is her father."

Robert Cassatt made a comfortable living as a stockbroker and real estate investor. His real estate activities set a curious pattern for family life during Mary's early years. Robert was a restless man, never content to stay in one place for long. He kept his family constantly on the move as he bought and sold property in Pittsburgh, Allegheny City, and Philadelphia.

In 1846 he served as mayor of Allegheny City and then spent two years on the city's Select Council. But important jobs were not enough to make Mr. Cassatt settle down. As head of the family, he was used to getting his way, and in 1848 he uprooted his family twice. They moved from Allegheny City to Pittsburgh and from Pittsburgh to the countryside near the eastern end of the state.

Even Katherine's patience must have worn thin as she moved to still another new home—her fifth house in just fourteen years of marriage. Fortunately, the new house was a lovely one, set in the green farmland near Lancaster. It was called Hardwick.

Hardwick gave five-year-old Mary her first real taste of freedom and adventure. There she learned to drive a tandem (a two-seated carriage), and her father taught her how to ride a horse. Mr. Cassatt and Mary rode together often, beginning a tradition that would last for decades. Mary became a skilled and fearless horsewoman. She liked to race across the fields with the wind in her face.

In those early, happy days at Hardwick, Mary had little need for friends: She had her big brother Aleck. The two children were very close, and they had similar interests and pleasures. They spent hours in the barn with the farm animals. Together they explored the Pennsylvania hills, in rain or shine. Years later, Aleck remembered the fun: "Mary was always a great favorite of mine, I suppose because our tastes were a good deal alike. Whenever it was a question of a walk, or a ride or a gallop on horseback . . . Mary was always ready."

Aleck also recalled, "We used to have plenty of fights . . . but we very soon made friends again." The two lively young Cassatts had other traits in common: courage and complete determination. These qualities would some day help Mary and Aleck reach their chosen goals.

The Cassatts were an old, distinguished family—not an extremely rich one. But in the nineteenth century, a gracious, leisurely way of life was possible for families of comfortable means. Mary's parents were able to employ several servants. They were also able to afford two homes. So in 1849, keeping Hardwick as their summer house, the Cassatts moved to Philadelphia.

Bustling Philadelphia—it was the city that Mary Cassatt would always think of as her true home, even though she would live for more than fifty years in France. When the Cassatts settled there, much of America was still a wild stretch of prairie and forest. So Philadelphia was an exciting place indeed. This fast-paced city was the second largest in the country, after New York. It was a leader in the industrial revolution that was taking place in America.

Philadelphia's streets were newly lit by gas, and Mary admired their nighttime glow. Like all the houses in prosperous neighborhoods, the Cassatts' boasted indoor plumbing. And although horse-drawn cabs and sleighs still carried people from street to street, the smoking, roaring railroad was rapidly surrounding the city. Philadelphia had other wonders, too. The Cassatt children were taken to gaze at the city's first skyscraper—an awesome eight stories high!

In her Philadelphia home, Mary met an artist for the first time. Her father asked the painter James Lambdin, whom he had known since boyhood, to paint a portrait of his three sons. All the Cassatt children crowded around the friendly

Philadelphia in the mid-1800s

Lambdin as he set up his easel and paints. Lydia and Mary watched curiously as their brothers posed. As the lifelike faces of Aleck, Robbie, and Gard appeared on the canvas, young Mary was amazed.

But an adventure even more exciting than life in Philadelphia awaited Mary: It was time to move again. Mr. Cassatt had decided to take a break from his business and was planning a long family stay in Europe to further Aleck's schooling. As Mary later observed, "Our father did not have at all the soul of a businessman. . . . He devoted himself to our education."

Mary's parents also hoped to find in Europe better medical care for Robbie, who suffered from a serious bone disease. The Cassatts prepared for the ocean crossing, which would take almost two weeks. In the fall of 1851, seven-year-old Mary sailed with her family toward the unknown—Paris, France.

Chapter Two

"A Passion for Line and Color"

"Well, Louis' done it!" cried Robert Cassatt as he dashed into his family's Paris apartment. The Cassatts had been in France only a few months. Now they heard shooting in the streets. Louis Napoléon, president of the French Republic, had just seized greater power. In 1852 he declared himself Emperor Napoléon III, and France's Second Empire began.

In the years to come, the Second Empire would bring much sorrow to France. But at present, many people, including the Cassatts, were happy that the emperor had started to modernize Paris. Louis Napoléon and his chief builder, Baron Haussmann, created lovely public parks and planted countless chestnut trees. They improved the city's sewer system in order to slow the spread of the awful disease cholera. And they turned narrow, ancient streets into wide boulevards. (In a few years, artists would sit in the cafés that lined those boulevards and talk about another kind of revolution—the revolution in painting.)

True to their restless pattern, the Cassatts left Paris and traveled by train to live in Prussia (part of what is now Germany). Aleck had shown great promise in the field of engineering, and Prussia's schools offered him the best technical training. In Heidelberg, Aleck entered boarding school. Soon the family moved with him to the town of Darmstadt for more specialized courses.

As Mary knew, her parents really were devoted to the education of all their children. But at the time, formal schooling was mostly for boys. Like many of their friends, Mary and her sister, Lydia, were tutored at home by a governess. While boys from well-to-do families prepared for profitable careers, their sisters concentrated on the skills they would need as homemakers and mothers. The extent of a young girl's education depended very much on the sensitivity and goals of her parents.

Mrs. Cassatt probably would have agreed with a female journalist who wrote in 1847: "The civilization of the world is to be the work of woman." Because Katherine loved learning, she filled her house with books. She took her daughters to museums and concerts. At an early age, Mary Cassatt became interested in the world outside her home. So while Aleck studied engineering, Mary explored old cobblestoned streets and learned to speak German. The foreign sights and sounds of Europe added to her feeling of wonder.

While still in Heidelberg, Mr. Cassatt commissioned another family portrait, and this time ten-year-old Mary was included. An artist named Peter Baumgaertner depicted Robbie and his father playing chess, with Gard and Mary standing nearby. In the drawing, Mary's hair is tied back neatly with ribbons, and she is wearing a velvet dress with a lace collar. Her wide-set eyes have a thoughtful, serious expression that makes her look older than her years.

This was to be the last family portrait to include Robbie Cassatt. The best doctors in France and Prussia had been unable to cure his bone disease. In Darmstadt, the twelve-year-old boy died, after years of pain. Mr. Cassatt wrote about Robbie in the family records: "He suffered very severely at times. . . . Dear, dear Boy! how gentle and good he was!" (Mary never forgot her brother. Robbie was buried in Darmstadt, but many years later, she would have him reburied in the family tomb in France.)

The Cassatts stopped briefly in Paris in 1855

before returning to America. Perhaps the dazzle of their favorite city distracted them for a moment from their terrible grief. It was the year of the Exposition Universelle (the World's Fair). Emperor Napoléon and the beautiful, red-haired Empress Eugénie held the huge fair to show the world the glory of France under their rule. Military bands and parades filled the streets. Houses were draped with colorful flags. Queen Victoria of England came, bringing members of her family, and a million more people flocked to Paris to see the sights.

Was it in Paris that young Mary Cassatt really felt the excitement, the importance of painting? The French took their art seriously. They were proud of their country's traditional place at the head of world culture. Great paintings expressed French values and boosted French prestige. Because of this, the 1855 Exposition had a special pavilion just for art. Mary and her family dressed in their best clothes to join the curious crowds there.

And at the art pavilion, tempers were hot! The French loved a good argument as much as they loved a good painting. People were choosing sides between two popular artists of the day—Jean-Auguste-Dominique Ingres and Eugène Delacroix.

Ingres painted in a classical style, with carefully drawn lines and well-outlined forms. His compositions (arrangement of objects in the picture) were always balanced. But the romantic Delacroix preferred to paint what art historian Phoebe Pool called a "river of movement" rather than a balanced composition. He loved bright color more than he loved line. Delacroix wrote in his journal, "Grey is the enemy of all painting. . . . Banish all earth colours."

The debate over classical *line* and romantic *color* was lively, and Mary enjoyed the thrill of the exhibit. But she was only eleven years old when she saw the paintings of Ingres and Delacroix. She had no way of knowing how important art would be to her some day. Nor did she realize that a young man who also saw the exhibit—Edgar Degas—would one day change her life.

❖ ❖ ❖

As a teenager back in Pennsylvania, Mary thought a lot about her life. Her friends were looking forward to marriage. In the meantime, they played tennis and went boating and horseback riding. In bonnets and elegant long dresses, they visited each other for tea. At night, they went to the theater.

But Mary felt a growing desire to paint. She wanted to make art her career. She worked hard to convince her father that she needed formal training, pointing out that more and more young women were attending art school. (To be sure, their accomplishments were admired but were not supposed to lead to a profession.) Mr. Cassatt gave his permission, probably hoping that a few years at school would dampen his daughter's enthusiasm.

Sixteen-year-old Mary was so anxious to study art that she signed up for classes six months ahead of time. In the fall of 1860 she entered the Pennsylvania Academy of the Fine Arts, in Philadelphia. There her enthusiasm did not fade; it burned brighter. She was delighted to be with other young people who loved art; she was especially pleased to be able to tell her parents that 30 percent of the students were women.

Mary and her new friend Eliza Haldeman called their school "the Cad." The oldest art school in America, it was housed in a beautiful Greek-style building, with tall columns and a dome. The school's curriculum followed the plan of the European art academies. In their quest to become artists, the students were required to follow a specific course of study.

The first two years were spent developing drawing skills, with emphasis on the human figure. Only after they had mastered drawing could students progress to painting and sculpture. In the beginning, Mary and Eliza drew from plaster casts of ancient sculptures and from live models. To perfect their understanding of the human body, they attended anatomy classes at Philadelphia's medical college. And like the other students, the two girls paid a fee for additional private lessons from artists on the academy's staff.

But Mary Cassatt wanted to learn everything—and quickly. She resented the Cad's rule that students must wait until their third year to paint. So she promptly began on her own, copying a large oil painting in the school's collection. There was an even more annoying rule, which deprived female students of valuable figure-drawing experience: Women were not allowed to enroll in the nude model class. (It was not until 1868 that this important course was finally opened to women.)

But the restrictions did not discourage Mary. She was soon one of the Cad's best students. Her confidence grew along with her training, and she felt set apart from those students who were amateurs "dabbling in paints." When Mary was nineteen, she imagined her works selling for $1,000 apiece. "Picture it—think of it!" she wrote to Eliza during a school break. Mary's dream was beginning to take shape.

As she worked hard, Mary also was determined to sample the pleasures offered in what she called the "good city of P." Horse-drawn trolleys took the art students everywhere. There were concerts in the magnificent new Academy of Music and picnics in Fairmount Park. Mary, Eliza, and Thomas Eakins, who would himself become a well-known painter, often went to art galleries to see what the dealers were selling. They also visited the city's mansions to view the paintings owned by Philadelphia's richest families. The Pennsylvania Academy itself held international art exhibitions, which attracted people from all over.

Philadelphia was truly a hub of activity. Its population was growing fast, and new businesses and factories were springing up daily. Such an industrial city had an important role to play in a growing nation, and it also had a role to play in war. The Civil War began on April 12, 1861, when the first shot was fired at Fort Sumter, in Charleston, South Carolina. Because of its excellent railway system, Philadelphia soon became a center for transporting Union soldiers and supplies. No battles were fought in the city, but the issues raised by the war were constantly discussed. Eliza Haldeman wrote about her hopes that slavery would be "abolished before the war is ended."

The Civil War ended in 1865. By that time, Mary felt that she had absorbed all that Philadelphia had to offer. The city had more fine pictures than most American communities, but after four years at school, Mary had seen them all. And like most serious art students, she wanted to

Women students at the Academy sewing a flag at the beginning of the Civil War

improve her technique by copying masterpieces. As she later told her first biographer, Achille Ségard, she realized that "one does not need to follow the lessons of an instructor. The teaching of museums is sufficient."

The great museums, with works by Old Masters such as Rubens and Velázquez, were across the ocean—in Europe. Mary was determined to see them. Mr. and Mrs. Cassatt worried about sending their daughter so far away, but to their credit, they allowed her to go. They realized that art was to be much more than a hobby for her. So in 1865, Mary traveled once again to Paris, the art capital of the Western world. She knew that she had been "born into the world with a passion for line and color." And she was eager to see where this passion would lead.

Chapter Three

Finding the Way

Twenty-one-year-old Mary Cassatt loved Paris. Napoléon III's builders had made it, in the words of one contemporary Parisian, "the brightest, airiest, and most beautiful of all cities." After she had settled in with friends of her parents, Mary went exploring. She walked along the sunny boulevards, admiring chestnut trees and pale marble buildings. Paris was a long way from Philadelphia. It was a new world, a world where beauty—and art—really mattered.

Eliza Haldeman and Thomas Eakins had also rushed to Paris after the Civil War. In fact, so many American art students had arrived that Eliza felt they were a distraction. She complained to her sister that there was too much "talking and amusing ourselves." Eliza and Mary were anxious to get to work.

The best art academy in Paris was the famous

École des Beaux-Arts (School of Fine Arts). Thomas Eakins enrolled right away. But Mary and Eliza could not, because women were not admitted. This rule was in strange contrast to the policy of the good old Pennsylvania Academy, where a large number of the students were women.

For Mary, obstacles were made to be overcome. She began private lessons with an extremely popular artist, Jean-Léon Gérôme. She also took instruction from the fashionable painter Charles Chaplin, who held a studio class "for ladies."

But Mary's favorite "school" was the Louvre, one of the world's largest art museums. It was a treasure trove of wonderful pictures, everything she had dreamed of back in Philadelphia. She set up her easel in the long halls of the museum and spent hours there, copying paintings by Old Masters. This was better than any art school. Mary knew that the great artists of the past would help her find a style of her own.

In Paris, "proper" painting style was dictated by the Academy, an elite group of professional artists. This group advised the French government on all matters concerning art. It decided what was "art" and what was not. The group, which had a tight grip on the art world, had been powerful since the late 1600s.

Academy officials ran the École des Beaux-

Arts and taught there, too. They decided which young people should be accepted at the school (certainly not women!). They also planned exactly what the students should learn.

The Academy teachers favored the classical style of Ingres, whose work stressed expressive *line* rather than brilliant *color*. Students were taught a traditional drawing and painting technique called *chiaroscuro*, which means "light-dark" in Italian. This was a method for carefully balanced shading—from the lightest tones to the darkest—to make objects in a picture appear to have three-dimensional form. Like the students at the Cad, École students were required to learn to draw before they could paint. When they were permitted to paint, they used mainly the approved earth colors (shades of black, brown, tan). Their brush strokes had to be well blended for a smooth look. And each painting was finished in the studio according to certain definite stages.

The Academy cared *how* an artist painted; it also had strong ideas about *what* should be painted. The professors thought that pictures should make people feel noble and lift them up from their daily lives. Academics liked to see scenes from the Bible, gods and goddesses from ancient myths, and heroic generals dashing into battle.

Even the human body should be improved

upon, they believed. One well-known teacher complained of the "ugly, enormous feet" that a student named Claude Monet was painting. "When one draws a figure," he told the young Monet, "one should always think of the antique. Nature, my friend, is all right as an element of study, but it offers no interest. Style, you see, is everything."

Style *was* almost everything to the men of the Academy, and they felt that they knew best what was beautiful and true. Once a year they formed a jury to select paintings to be displayed at a Paris art show called the Salon. This large exhibition was the official marketplace of French art: Prizes were awarded, and artists' reputations were made or destroyed. In nineteenth-century Paris, there were very few other places where paintings could be sold. So most artists tried hard to be accepted by the jury—if they wanted to make a living.

And if the jury didn't like a painting? It was rejected. One year a record 4,000 pictures were turned away! A growing number of artists bitterly resented the Academy's absolute power. Among those who protested were two painters whom Mary Cassatt admired very much—Gustave Courbet and Edouard Manet. These two men boycotted the 1867 Salon and set up private exhibitions of their own.

Courbet was the leader of the Realist movement in art. He painted scenes of the rural life near his home instead of events from history or myth. The Academy disapproved of Courbet's pictures of peasants going about their daily work. His realistic approach was too casual, too crude for them.

And what did the conservative men of the Academy think of Manet's painting *Le Déjeuner sur l'herbe (Luncheon on the Grass)*? They were shocked. They thought that Manet's brushwork was fuzzy and that his figures were flat (no *chiaroscuro*). And who but a crazy man would paint naked people at a picnic? Manet's pictures had to be protected by armed guards. They had to be hung high on the wall so people couldn't beat them with their umbrellas. The poor artist wrote to a friend, "Insults rain down on me like hailstones."

Manet was sad that the Salon often rejected and jeered at his work. He wanted to win the Academy's approval. But he stuck to his principles: "There is only one true thing: instantly paint what you see. When you've got it, you've got it. When you haven't, begin again."

Manet was not alone. More and more young painters wanted to be freed from the old rules. There was room for more than one kind of art, they reasoned. Sipping wine in the cafés of Paris, the artists talked about painting the ordinary life that bustled around them.

Manet's Le Déjeuner sur l'herbe (Luncheon on the Grass), *which scandalized the French art world*

Eliza Haldeman wrote home about the conflicts in the Paris art world: "The French school is going through a phase. . . . just now everything is Chaos." For fresh ideas and fresh air, Mary Cassatt and Eliza left Paris to paint in the countryside.

They joined a small colony of landscape painters in Courances, which Eliza described as a "little, out of the way French village." The quaint rural life there was an adventure for the two young women. "Everything [was] in the most primitive style," wrote Eliza. They worked on their paintings and explored the area, with its park and its old château. In Courances they even learned how to make French candy—and laughed about "getting fat."

Their next stop was the village of Ecouen, where artists were concentrating on genre painting (scenes of everyday life). Here Mary worked hard on her figure-painting skills. In another of her letters home, Eliza described the humorous side of trying to paint people: "Our little models tease us nearly to death, sing, dance, and cut up all sorts of capers."

Figure painting paid off for Mary. At Ecouen she painted *La Mandoline (The Mandolin Player)*, a study of a young female musician in a thoughtful mood. This picture, in the traditional style, was Mary's first work to gain official recognition. For reasons she never explained, she submitted it to the Paris Salon under a name she would use professionally for the next six years—"Miss Mary Stevenson." (Stevenson, Mary's middle name, was also the surname of her maternal grandmother.) To her joy, the painting was accepted.

One of Eliza Haldeman's paintings was also accepted at the Salon. The two friends traveled to Paris for the thrill of seeing their work on display. A writer for the *New York Times* praised Mary's *La Mandoline* for its "vigor of treatment and fine qualities of color." And the same writer called Eliza a young artist of "unmistakeable talent."

But Eliza's thoughts kept turning to America. She wrote to her family, "I am constantly dreaming that I am at home." At the end of 1868, she said good-bye to Mary and returned to Philadelphia, where she later married. Perhaps Eliza became distracted or found that art was too demanding, for there is no record of any more paintings by Mary's good friend.

Mary Cassatt, however, was just getting started. A second oil painting was accepted by the Salon in 1870. Her ambition was strong, and she joked that she wanted to paint even better than the Old Masters. But she knew that she still had much to learn. She continued to travel to out-of-the-way places, not minding "dirt and fleas" as long as she found interesting subjects to paint.

Mary was looking for a studio in Paris when her European stay came to an abrupt halt. On July 19, 1870, Napoléon III declared war on Prussia. The painter Edouard Manet spoke for many people when he said, "I believe that we unhappy Parisians are going to play the parts of actors in something dreadful. It will be death, fire, plunder, carnage, if [the rest of] Europe does not arrive in time to stop it." The war could not be stopped, however, and France was about to become a dangerous place to be. Reluctantly, Mary boarded the ship for the safety of home.

Chapter Four

Old Masters and a New Art

While Mary Cassatt was in Pennsylvania, Louis Napoléon's Second Empire crumbled. In 1870 the Prussians laid siege to Paris, and the city was cut off from the rest of the world. Mail could leave Paris only by hot-air balloon. Smallpox broke out. Although French soldiers and citizens tried to defend the city, the situation was hopeless.

Parisians began to starve. Instead of vegetables, they boiled weeds from their gardens. After they had eaten all the cows, sheep, cats, and dogs they could find, the people were forced to kill and eat the animals in the zoo. Bear meat and elephants' trunks were sold in the butcher shops. Victor Hugo, the famous author of *Les Misérables*, even wrote a cookbook with a recipe for rat pie.

The Prussians quickly defeated France's army. Napoléon III was taken prisoner and wrote to Empress Eugénie about his country's downfall: "I never dreamed of a catastrophe so appalling." By 1871 a new French government, the Third Republic, had been formed so that a peace treaty with the victorious Prussians could be signed.

Mary knew that she was lucky to have escaped Paris, but the interruption of her career was torture for her. She settled with her sister and parents in Altoona, Pennsylvania, to be near Aleck and his young wife, Lois, niece of President Buchanan. Altoona, which was then the headquarters of the Pennsylvania Railroad, was a temporary stop for Aleck in his career as a successful railroad magnate. But the town offered nothing for an ambitious young artist.

Twenty-six-year-old Mary had already had two pictures accepted at the Paris Salon. She had met talented painters and seen many of the art treasures of Europe. Now, in Altoona, she could barely find the canvases and colors that she needed. And good models for her paintings were also scarce. (When her father tried to sit for her, he often fell asleep.)

In a fit of frustration, Mary wrote to Emily Sartain, a fellow Philadelphian and artist: "I have given up my studio & torn up my father's portrait, & have not touched a brush for six weeks." Mary longed for Europe. "My eyes water to see a fine picture again," she told her friend. Thirty-year-old Emily, already a professional engraver, wanted to learn to paint. She agreed with Cassatt that they must get back to Europe at all costs.

Money was the problem. Mr. Cassatt had insisted that Mary pay her own studio and travel expenses, but Mary lacked the funds to do so. She had been unable to sell a single painting, either in Pennsylvania or in New York.

It was not in Mary Cassatt's nature to give up, though. She told Emily Sartain, "Patience is my motto," and traveled with two cousins to Chicago. Hoping to attract attention, Mary placed her pictures in the window of the city's largest jewelry store.

Her timing could not have been worse. The Great Chicago Fire of 1871, the worst in the city's history, broke out. For twenty-four hours it raged. Mary's work went up in ash and smoke. Relieved that his sister and cousins had escaped with their lives, Aleck wrote to Lois Cassatt: "My Dear Little Wife, They are now back at Pittsburgh, saved the baggage, but Mary's pictures were lost. I am glad they got off so easily."

Her return to Pittsburgh brought Mary the good luck that she needed. Bishop Michael Domenec wanted paintings to decorate his cathedral, but he couldn't afford original masterpieces. He gave Mary a commission to go to Parma, Italy, to copy two works by the sixteenth-century

Italian master Correggio.

Now that she had money from the commission, Mary wrote to Emily, "I am wild to be off, I have lost too much time already." Not even the horrible seasickness that she suffered could hold her back. (She spent every ocean crossing in her cabin and usually had to be carried off the boat.) With Emily as her travel companion, Mary set off on her third trip to Europe. In Italy she hoped to pick up where she had left off.

Parma was off the beaten track for tourists, and the Italians warmly welcomed the two American women. Mary and Emily shared a beautifully furnished room in what Emily described as an "old palazzo [palace] with an angel frescoed in the centre panel of [the] very high ceiling." Their landlady went out of her way to make them comfortable, and expenses were not high. Day began early, with coffee and good bread served in front of the fire. The evening meal was delicious, too, with red wine and "innumerable varieties of maccaroni."

Sightseeing was a joy. Mary and Emily went for carriage rides and took long walks at sunset. There were centuries-old churches to see and buildings of rose-colored brick. Emily wrote home, "Parma grows upon us more and more,—its picturesqueness is developed wonderfully by the bright sun." Carrying a parasol to keep the sun off her face,

Mary soaked up the atmosphere like a sponge.

Although the women did not speak Italian well, they made friends easily. Their closest friend was Carlo Raimondi, who was professor of engraving at Parma's academy of art. With Raimondi's help, the two Philadelphians were soon included in the social life of the city. The professor escorted them to dinner parties and the opera and even located a horse for Mary to ride. Best of all, he provided the women with a well-lighted studio at the academy, free of charge. Mary called him "that angel."

The commission from the bishop of Pittsburgh opened a new door for Mary. As she put it, "For eight months I went to school to Correggio—a prodigious Master." This Italian artist, who had lived more than three hundred years earlier, had a profound effect on Mary. His lifelike babies and natural-looking Madonnas (mothers of Christ) found a special place in her heart. In the quiet old churches of Parma, Mary climbed tall ladders so that she could copy the Correggios on the domed ceilings.

The bishop was pleased with the results of Mary's work and paid her even more than she had asked. But as always, Cassatt was highly critical of her own skill. Before she sent one painting back to Pittsburgh, she confided to Emily, "My copy is

Mary, age 28, in a photograph taken in Parma, Italy

nearly done... & it looks 'beastly'—I am more and more disgusted with it."

In reality, Mary's work was far from "beastly." Her new paintings were more sophisticated than her earlier work had been. *Two Women Throwing Flowers During Carnival* attracted favorable attention. In this picture, Mary combined traditional technique with the modern theme of a joyful carnival.

Emily Sartain wrote to her father about Mary's rapid progress. "All Parma is talking of Miss Cassatt and her picture, and everyone is anxious to know her—The compliments she receives are overwhelming." Even a professor at the Parma academy came to Mary for advice.

Emily took her friend's greater talent in good spirit, adding in her letter, "I shine a little, by [Mary's] reflection." And Cassatt had always encouraged her in her work. But Emily was not as interested as Mary was in Parma's Old Masters. It was time for her to move on. Emily took the train to Paris, where she began to study with a popular artist of the Salon.

Mary was lonely without Emily Sartain. But it seemed that Cassatt could never see enough great paintings and that her wanderings would never end. She had inherited her mother's curiosity, as well as her father's love of travel. In the fall of

1872, she traveled alone to Spain, visiting the cities of Madrid and Seville. As Edouard Manet had earlier, Mary found inspiration in the Spanish museums. She wrote to Emily in Paris, "Although I think now that Correggio is perhaps the greatest painter that ever lived, these Spaniards make a much greater impression *at first*."

The pictures by Velázquez stopped Mary in her tracks. To Emily in Paris she wrote, "Velázquez oh! my but you knew how to paint!" His work was more alive than any she had ever seen. "The men and women have a reality about them which exceed anything I ever supposed possible. . . . Why you can walk into the picture[s]."

Mary was awed; she felt "like a miserable little 'critter'" when she compared her skill with that of Velázquez. Yet she learned all she could from his style. The result was several vigorous paintings of toreadors and women in traditional Spanish costumes, some of Cassatt's best early work.

Slowly but surely, the young woman from Philadelphia was making a name for herself. One of Mary's paintings received the honor of being hung "on the line" (at eye level) at the Paris Salon of 1872. Since many pictures were hung so high that they were practically invisible, she was delighted.

The Cassatt family, back in Philadelphia, was also delighted by this unexpected success. Yet mixed with their pride was a feeling of worry about their "headstrong" Mary. A career in art was a risky thing. It could bring fame, but it could also end in failure and a broken heart.

Aleck Cassatt felt as close as always to his sister. Before his marriage, he had written about Mary to his future wife: "I want you to know her." Now he spoke for the whole family when he wrote again to Lois, "Mary is in high spirits as her picture has been accepted for the annual exhibition in Paris. You must understand that this is a great honor for a young artist and not only has it been accepted but it has been 'hung on the line.' I don't know what that means but I suppose it means it has been hung in a favorable position. Mary's art name is 'Mary Stevenson' under which name I suppose she expects to become famous, poor child."

In 1874, after further travels in Europe, Mary Cassatt "came home" to Paris. She found that the city had recovered from the Franco-Prussian War and was sparkling with life. The new government, the Third Republic, had quickly paid its war debts to the Prussians. People were again swarming to Paris to visit and to live, as they had in Napoléon III's days. One Parisian compared the crowds of people and horse-drawn carriages to an "overflowing river."

The tremendous growth in population brought

growth in commerce, too. New hotels, restaurants, and cafés sprang up. Wealthy Parisians filled the theaters and shopped in the new fashionable department stores that lined the boulevards. There they bought, as one tourist exuberantly described it, luxurious "porcelains, perfumery, bronzes, carpets, furs, mirrors . . . the most aristocratic beer, and the best flavored coffee."

Yet there were people who missed the old, quaint Paris that had existed before the Second Empire. They hated Napoléon III for having demolished so much of it. And they felt that the city had lost its soul to the modern, businesslike spirit. In Mary Cassatt's view, this commercialism, with its emphasis on money, had also hurt the art world. But after years of travel and study, she realized that Paris was the best place for a painter to build a reputation and to sell pictures.

Within a year, Mary had settled at 19, rue de Laval. She began to see acquaintances from her earlier days in the city. She also added new friends to her social circle. Mary loved to talk, and there were soon many visitors at her studio. They came to drink *chocolat* and to argue about politics, literature, and, of course, painting.

At first, Emily Sartain and Mary Cassatt were glad to see each other again. Emily wrote to her family, "Oh how good it is to be with some one who talks understandingly and enthusiastically about Art." The two friends discussed the struggle between academic painting and the more realistic type of art that was influenced by Gustave Courbet and Edouard Manet.

Cassatt's opinions were strong. She was losing respect for the stuffy traditions of the Academy and preferred the painters of modern life to the artists of the Salon. Mary was fascinated by Courbet and Manet. She was also becoming interested in the younger "rebels," Monet and Renoir.

But Emily was still studying with a Salon painter. Although she agreed somewhat with Mary, she thought her friend's ideas were too rebellious. She explained to her father, "I by no means agree with all of Miss C's judgments,—she is entirely too slashing, . . . disdains the salon pictures . . . and all the names we are used to revere."

The friendship suffered from the same disagreements that were dividing the rest of Paris's art community. In a short time, misunderstanding and rivalry led to bitterness. Mary snubbed Emily, thinking that her friend had criticized her work behind her back. Furious at this treatment, Emily wrote that Mary was "very touchy and selfish." The close relationship came to an end.

The next few years brought Mary Cassatt another conflict as well. She was torn between her need to sell pictures at the Salon and her natural desire for a more independent style of painting. She went through a period of great self-doubt. In later years, Mary would write, "When I came to live in Paris . . . the sight of the annual exhibitions quite led me astray. I thought I must be wrong & the painters admired of the public right."

Cassatt painted a number of Academic-style "crowd pleasers," and they sold well. But she also began to experiment with lighter colors and looser brushwork. She soon found out that past successes at the Salon were no guarantee of future acceptance. These new, more daring pictures were rejected. May Alcott, sister of the famous Louisa May Alcott, author of *Little Women*, thought that Mary's work now showed "too original a style for these fogies [of the Salon] to appreciate."

In 1875, when one of her paintings was turned down, Mary suspected that its background had been judged "too light." To test her theory, she darkened the colors and resubmitted the altered picture one year later. It was promptly accepted by the Salon jury. Angry at being told how to paint, Cassatt wondered whether the price of success was too high.

Mary shared her independent ideas with an American friend named Louisine Elder, who was at boarding school in Paris. Although Louisine was ten years younger than Mary, the two became as close as sisters. They had in common a love for beautiful paintings and happily roamed Paris together in search of them.

Many years later, when Louisine had become the fabulously wealthy Mrs. Henry O. Havemeyer, she remembered seeing a Courbet painting with Mary. In her memoirs she wrote, "Miss Cassatt . . . explained Courbet to me, spoke of the great painter in her flowing and generous way, called my attention to his marvelous execution, to his color, above all to his realism. . . . I recall her saying to me . . . 'it lives, it is almost too real.'"

One day Cassatt walked down a Paris street and saw an unusual picture in a shop window. It was Edgar Degas's *La Répétition de Ballet (The Ballet Rehearsal)*. She stood in front of it for a long time. Degas's ballerinas were vividly drawn and their movements seemed so real. Mary felt that the artist had caught forever the truth of a single moment.

The pastel made such an impression on her that she urged Louisine to buy it, for she could not afford it herself. Her best friend shared Mary's excitement and gladly spent all of her savings—$100—on Degas's dancers. Thus in 1875, Louisine Elder became the first American to own a picture by Edgar Degas. And Degas, whose family was sunk in debt, was deeply grateful for the sale.

Degas's The Ballet Rehearsal *captivated Cassatt and changed the way she thought about art.*

Mary Cassatt could see that Degas painted to please himself and no one else. His pastel was completely original. His courage to be different struck a chord in Mary's soul, and she realized that she, too, had the courage to keep on experimenting. She never forgot that day. When she was old, Mary wrote to Louisine about seeing *La Répétition de Ballet*: "How well I remember, nearly forty years ago, seeing for the first time Degas' pastels in the window of a picture dealer.... I used to go and flatten my nose against that window and absorb all I could of his art. It changed my life."

Cassatt's Madame Cortier

Chapter Five

"There Is Someone Who Feels as I Do"

Mary Cassatt and Edgar Degas became aware of each other at almost the same time. Shortly before Mary saw his ballet dancers in a shop window, Degas strolled through the Paris Salon with his friend Joseph Tourny. He glanced at the hundreds of paintings lining the walls and was not impressed. Suddenly, he stopped in front of Mary's picture, entitled *Madame Cortier*.

Degas liked this portrait of a middle-aged woman, with her richly colored hair, her twinkling eyes, and her slight smile. It showed the spark of originality. The painting was not a "society" portrait, designed to flatter the subject: It was realistic. The viewer could see Mme Cortier's personality shining through.

For the first time, the artist had signed her name "Mary Cassatt" instead of "Mary Stevenson."

Degas thought about the American woman Mary Cassatt, and said to Tourny, "It's true. There is someone who feels as I do."

And Edgar Degas's feelings about art were intense. He had a passion for painting what was real. He painted his subjects in casual poses so that their unique personalities could be seen. In his notebook, Degas jotted down, "If a person is a laughing type, make this person laugh."

But Parisian life interested him the most, and he wanted to paint every aspect of it. In Louisine Havemeyer's words, Degas's aim was to show things "no worse and no better than they were." He created a series of pictures on everything from ballerinas to jockeys, bassoon players to laundresses. And in every one of his paintings, Degas revealed his fascination with movement. His racehorses seem about to thunder off the canvas; his dancers' muscles strain with the effort of stretching.

Naturally, Degas despised the jury system. Like Cassatt, he felt that the traditions of the Salon had reached a dead end. Why shouldn't artists be free to paint exactly as they wished? Degas loved to discuss these issues. At the Café Guerbois, in the Montmartre district of Paris, he and other painters argued far into the night—and sometimes until breakfast.

The café was also the favorite hangout of

Manet, Monet, Renoir, Camille Pissarro, Alfred Sisley, and Paul Cézanne. (Cassatt did not go there because café life was considered improper for women.) Most of the artists had been rejected often by the Salon and agreed with Degas that the juries had no right to judge their work. They were sick of the dull pictures of kings and cupids approved by the Academy. They were sick of the dull earth colors, too. So they set about creating their own kind of art.

In his review of one Salon show, the poet Baudelaire had called for more modern paintings: "Life [in Paris] is rich in poetic and marvellous subjects. We are . . . in an atmosphere of the marvellous; but we do not notice it." Degas and his friends did notice it. They spoke of the artistic scandals created by Manet. They listened when Manet said, "I would show the Paris of the public markets, bridges . . . race courses and parks."

The young artists who met at the Café Guerbois were already painting modern Paris. As Renoir said, "There isn't a person, a landscape or a subject that doesn't possess at least some interest." A painter's job, he believed, was to "bring out [the] hidden treasure" in the everyday—cafés and railway stations, operagoers and barmaids.

Many of the rebels found inspiration in the countryside. Carrying easels and paints to picturesque spots along the Seine River, they painted all day in the open air. They were eager to observe nature as closely as possible. Not for them were the Salon landscapes, which were polished to perfection indoors. Monet, in particular, was devoted to nature. He and Renoir, who often set up their easels nearby each other, produced joyful scenes of flowering fields and boating parties on the sunny river.

More than anything, the young painters valued artistic freedom. But they knew that the Academy would not loosen its grip without a fight. In 1867 Courbet and Manet had bypassed the Salon and shown their paintings directly to the public. Now Degas and his friends decided to do the same. Vowing never again to submit pictures to the juries, they planned a separate exhibit of their work. The official name they chose for themselves was the "Anonymous Society of Artists, Painters, Sculptors, Engravers, etc." But Degas called the group, simply, the "Independents." In 1874 this bold new company of artists took a risky step into the future.

The group's first exhibit, held at a photographer's studio, sent shock waves through Paris. People were outraged that the artists seemed to be throwing out tradition. Their themes and techniques were so new that the critics immediately set about "devouring" them. A reporter for the Parisian newspaper *Le Figaro* wrote that their work reminded him "of a monkey who might have got hold of a box of paints." Another critic joked that the crazy pictures were causing people to bite each other in the streets!

Manet, still hoping that the Salon would come to appreciate his modern style, refused to join. But more than thirty artists were brave enough to participate in the exhibit. (Berthe Morisot was the only woman.) Their paintings, which had so upset the conservatives, depicted scenes from daily life—including a horse race (by Degas), Morisot's little daughter playing hide-and-seek, and a beautiful woman at the theater (by Renoir).

Claude Monet's painting *Impression: Sunrise* was singled out for ridicule. Most people had never seen anything like it before. They could not understand Monet's blurred outlines and splashes of color on the water. A mocking critic named Louis Leroy wrote, "A preliminary drawing for a wallpaper design is more highly finished than this seascape." He used the title of Monet's painting to give the Independents the label that would stick to them forever—the Impressionists.

Degas hated the label. He did not want to be identified with a single style of painting. Independence was all that mattered to him. Yet the name *Impressionist* made some sense. Camille Pissarro

Monet's Impression: Sunrise *was the source of the group's name—the Impressionists.*

spoke for many in the group when he told a student, "Don't proceed according to the rules and principles but paint what you observe and feel. . . . It is best not to lose the first impression."

Fortunately, not everyone laughed at the Impressionists. The Paris art dealer Paul Durand-Ruel believed in their work from the start and tried to sell their paintings when most people thought the new art was a joke. In 1876 Durand-Ruel hosted the Second Impressionist Exhibit, but it was just as badly received as the first. Conservative critic Albert Wolff called it a "frightening spectacle." In the newspaper *Le Figaro* he wrote, "Try to make M. Pissarro understand that trees are not violet, that the sky is not the color of fresh butter!"

Like Durand-Ruel, the young writer J. K. Huysmans recognized the need for change: "In a new age, new techniques. It's a simple matter of good sense." The Impressionists, Huysmans realized, had not only chosen different subjects to paint; they had figured out different ways to paint them.

For the first time, artists could paint outdoors with ease, thanks to new materials—ready-made canvases and portable tubes of paint. They could pack up their equipment and leave their studios to look at town and country with fresh eyes. Their paintings shimmered with light. They noticed that as the sun's light changes, the colors of the world change with it. And they saw colors that traditional Salon artists did not see. From firsthand observation, Impressionists realized that shadows were not always brown or black but reflected all the colors that swirled around them.

To make their pictures alive with color, the Impressionists paired pure red, yellow, and blue with their complementary colors—green, violet, and orange. To make their pictures sparkle, they used plenty of white. They favored the new ready-made canvases with pale backgrounds because patches of pale canvas showing through the paint gave an added effect of sunlight.

When they looked at the world, the Impressionists saw light and color and people and objects in constant motion. To capture this sense of movement, they often applied their paint thickly and painted rapidly: It was important to keep the inspiration of the first idea. Brush strokes were free, sometimes sketchy and broken. Outlines of objects were soft. These revolutionary artists just painted what they saw. They wondered, would the fuss ever die down?

But being ignored was just as bad as being fussed at. In these early years, many of the Impressionists could not sell their paintings. They were so poor that they could barely afford brushes and tubes of paint, and they had to borrow money from Durand-Ruel. (Years later Renoir claimed, "Without him we wouldn't have survived.") At one point, Renoir and Pissarro had to paint window blinds in order to eat. Pissarro wrote in 1878, "Art is a matter of a hungry belly, an empty purse, of poor luckless devils." And Monet was often frantic. He wrote to Manet, "Not a penny left since the day before yesterday and no more credit at the butcher's or the baker's. Even though I believe in the future, you can see that the present is very hard indeed." In their worst moods, some of the artists thought of returning to the Salon.

Not Degas. He was always on the lookout for new recruits for the group. One afternoon in 1877, the forty-three-year-old artist put on his starched white collar, his high black hat, and his silk cravat (necktie). He went to visit Mary Cassatt in her studio in hilly, cobblestoned Montmartre. The two artists greatly admired each other's work, but they had never met. And they had no way of knowing that Degas's visit would begin a friendship that would last for forty years.

Degas asked Cassatt to join the Impressionist movement. Mary, who had been watching their work with interest, didn't hesitate. She said yes. Many years later she remembered that day: "I accepted with joy. At last I could work with complete independence. . . . I hated conventional art. I began to live."

Why did the proper young woman from Philadelphia join a revolutionary group of artists? At thirty-three, Mary had a good reputation at the Salon and a steady income from the sale of her pictures. She had succeeded in a field where only a handful of women had before. Now, if she left the Salon, there could be no guarantee that anyone would buy—or even notice—her work.

Cassatt risked her career because she, too, believed that artists should work in freedom. The narrow-minded juries were stifling her powerful love of truth. By studying the Old Masters, she had developed her talent with painstaking care. Now she had the confidence to paint in the modern style, in the independent manner of the Impressionists. And Mary Cassatt had a pioneer spirit: She loved a new beginning.

❖ ❖ ❖

Tall, slender Mary Cassatt and aristocratic Edgar Degas found that they were kindred spirits. Their backgrounds, personalities, and ideas about art were remarkably similar. They had both been raised in well-to-do, cultured homes. (Degas's father had been a banker, Cassatt's an investor.) Their manners were formal, their appearances proper. When Degas went out, he was always perfectly groomed, and Mary's neatly tailored outfits and stylish hats came from the best dressmakers in Paris. Neither of the two artists was interested in mingling in wealthy social circles, though. They dined together and worked together, and preferred to spend their evenings in small gatherings, talking heatedly about politics, books, and art.

They became lifelong friends. Only someone as strong willed as Mary could have been unafraid of Degas. He was often difficult to be with, and his wit could be sarcastic and cruel. Of Berthe Morisot he said, "She makes pictures the way one would make a hat." To the American painter James McNeill Whistler he said, "If you were not a genius you would be the most ridiculous man in Paris." Degas saved his worst temper for art critics. It was even rumored that he threw one of them down the stairs!

Mary, too, was outspoken and expressed her likes and dislikes boldly. Her dry wit was a match for Degas's. And she understood the irritable genius, seeing past his bad moods to the loyal heart underneath. Later in life, Mary explained to Louisine Havemeyer how she had managed to get along with him. Her face lit up as she spoke of her "magnificent" but "dreadful" friend: "Oh, I am independent," she said. "I can live alone and I love to work. Sometimes it made him furious that he could not find a chink in my armor, and there would be months when we just could not see each other, and then something I painted would bring us together again."

From the very beginning, work brought the two together. In 1879 Degas did an etching of Mary leaning on her furled umbrella at the Louvre. She also posed trying on a hat for his picture *At the Milliner's*. As she explained to Louisine, "he finds the movement difficult, and the model cannot seem to get his idea." Mary even inspired Degas to write a sonnet and dedicate it to her.

When Mary joined the Impressionists, Degas began to advise her on her work. He knew that she was extremely gifted. Although Cassatt was Degas's friend—not his student—she learned more from him than she did from any other artist. Once he helped paint the background of one of her pictures. Completed in 1878, it was called *Little Girl in a Blue Armchair.*

The painting contains some clues about the two artists' special friendship. The little girl sprawled in the armchair was the daughter of friends of Degas. All the chairs are "cropped" (cut off) at the sides of the picture, almost as if they were in a snapshot. This is a technique that Cassatt learned from Degas, who was fascinated by the new medium of photography. And the little sleeping dog is a Belgian griffon, which Degas had found for Mary. He had asked the breeder to supply a dog for "this distinguished person whose friendship I honour. . . . It is a young dog that she needs, so that he may love her." (The dog was the first of many Belgian griffons that Mary would cherish throughout her life.)

While Cassatt eagerly learned from Degas, her originality was unmistakable. *Little Girl in a Blue Armchair* shows Mary's wonderful ability to capture a child's mood. Cassatt had no use for the stiff portraits of children that were so popular at the Salon.

She preferred to paint her subjects in more natural poses. The little girl in this picture looks bored and restless, as if she would much rather be out playing.

Because there was no Impressionist exhibit in 1878, Mary submitted *Little Girl in a Blue Armchair* to the American jury of that year's Exposition Universelle. She was thoroughly disgusted when the painting was rejected. Years later she recalled her anger: "Since M. Degas had thought it good I was furious especially because he had worked on it . . . and the jury consisted of three people, one of whom was a pharmacist!"

Both Degas and Cassatt were thought of as the "indoor" Impressionists because they rarely painted landscapes or worked in the open air. Instead, they concentrated on the moods and movements of people. The two friends were tireless workers who aimed at perfection. Mary usually arrived at her studio at 8 A.M. and stayed there until dark. As for Degas, he wrote, "I cannot stop putting the final touches to my pictures, pastels." He could take years to finish a single painting and sometimes reworked a picture until he had ruined it and had to throw it away.

"Beauty is a mystery," said Degas. And he and Mary devoted their lives to it. Neither of them ever married, probably fearing that a family would stand in the way of the work that they loved. In his notebook Degas explained, "If one wants to be a serious artist today and create an original little niche for oneself . . . one must constantly immerse oneself in solitude." He also observed that "a painter has no private life."

Yet the decision never to marry also brought regrets. In his loneliness, Degas would, he said, "often weep over my poor life." And in Cassatt's old age, she spoke sadly of the sacrifices she had made to become a great painter: "My mistake was in not having children."

Were Mary Cassatt and Edgar Degas in love? No one knows. After Degas died, Mary burned all their letters. Their feelings for each other were certainly profound. But, like beauty, their relationship remains a mystery.

Chapter Six

Mary Cassatt, Impressionist

The Cassatts did not want Mary to live alone. And Mary's father, now seventy-one, was ready to retire from his brokerage firm, Lloyd and Cassatt. So in 1877 he and Mrs. Cassatt and Lydia came to Paris to live, while Aleck, Lois, and Gard stayed behind in Philadelphia.

Mary left 19, rue de Laval and moved with her family to 13, avenue Trudaine, an apartment near her studio. The new, larger apartment, with its sixth-floor balcony, commanded a splendid view of the city. Happy with the arrangement, the hard-to-please Mr. Cassatt wrote home to Aleck, "Paris is a wonder to behold."

Paris, truly the favorite city of all the Cassatts, was an exciting place to live during retirement. Soon after Mary's parents and sister arrived, there was another Exposition Universelle, staged to celebrate France's recovery from the Franco-Prussian War. (This was the same Exposition that rejected Mary's painting *Little Girl in a Blue Armchair*.) The World's Fair brought back memories of the one the family had seen in 1855, and it provided endless entertainment. The entire city was on holiday, with neighborhoods competing to display the most festive decorations, the brightest flags. In a letter to Aleck's family, Katherine Cassatt wrote, "We would have liked so much to have you all with us to see the beautiful fireworks and illuminations which were much finer than those you can see in America." Robert wrote to his oldest grandchild, Eddie Cassatt, about the "thousand and one . . . delights" of his new home. He told Aleck that the Exposition was ending in a "blaze of glory."

When the fair was over and the commotion had died down, Cassatt family life began to take on much the same shape it had back in Philadelphia. Mary was swept up in its routine. There was tea with Lydia and shopping with her mother. She often accompanied her father on his daily six-mile walk. And as in the old days, Mary and her father went riding. Instead of galloping over the Pennsylvania hills, they rode in the grand Bois de Boulogne, at the city's edge. This forested park, with its ponds and winding pathways, attracted a fashionable crowd in search of recreation.

But a family as close as the Cassatts could not be completely happy unless they were all together. The Paris Cassatts missed the Philadelphia Cassatts terribly. Through dozens of letters, Mary, Lydia, and their parents tried to stay in touch. They were disappointed that "Gard writes very meagre letters," but had better luck with Aleck and his family. Even the smallest details about Aleck's four young children were a source of delight. "Grandmamma Cassatt" wrote to her granddaughter Katharine: "Yesterday I received your very nice letter which your Aunt Mary & I read over several times & which we thought extremely good for a little girl not yet seven years old. You cannot want to see me more than I wish to see you."

For Mary, living with her family again was both a joy and a burden. Her parents were elderly, and forty-year-old Lydia, who was suffering from a kidney ailment called Bright's disease, was almost an invalid. Therefore, household tasks and decisions and even travel plans were responsibilities that fell on Mary's capable shoulders. As much as she loved her family, what Mary really wanted to do was paint. Caught between home life and the revolutionary art movement she had just joined, Cassatt struggled to balance the two worlds.

She succeeded. Mary Cassatt's family became

an excellent source of models for her. They were enthusiastic, available—and free. In their effort to record everyday life, Impressionists frequently painted family members as they ate lunch, read the papers, or brushed their hair. This custom suited Mary well, since her family was usually no farther away than the next room. As she prepared for her first show with the Impressionists, her work blossomed. Mr. Cassatt was able to report, "Mame is working away as diligently as ever." In spite of their claims on her time, Mary's family was inspiring her to paint some of her most radiant pictures.

Lydia, whom Mary cherished, was a favorite model. She is the subject of *Lydia in a Loge, Wearing a Pearl Necklace*, painted in 1879. This masterpiece is one of Cassatt's first truly Impressionist paintings because it is bursting with light and color. Lydia sits in a red velvet chair at the Paris Opera House. She is wearing a delicious dress, the color of pink icing and trimmed with lace. Her pearls gleam white and a chandelier sheds golden light on her hair. Behind her a mirror reflects the glittering scene, and Lydia is smiling.

In this picture, Mary used her Impressionist's ability to capture one shining moment, what is sometimes called a slice of life. Like Degas and Renoir, Cassatt loved the theater and took her sketchbook there often. The new Opera House, completed in 1875, was one of the most majestic buildings planned during the Second Empire. With its sparkling chandeliers and miles of mirrors, it was a glamorous gathering place for modern Parisian society. But while Degas focused mostly on the performers on stage and in the wings, Cassatt was intrigued by the audience. In a series of theater pictures, Mary portrayed women in expensive box seats, enjoying the spectacle around them. These were her friends and relatives; she painted the world that she knew.

Lydia in a Loge, Wearing a Pearl Necklace and ten other pictures by Cassatt were shown at the Fourth Impressionist Exhibit, in 1879. This was Mary's first exhibit with the Impressionists, and she had worked feverishly for two years in order to be ready. The show was held at 28, avenue de l'Opéra, from April 10 to May 11. Fifteen other artists took part. Mary was—and always would be—the only American in the group. For this exhibit, she was also the only woman, because Berthe Morisot was home awaiting the birth of her baby.

Mary had joined the movement at an exciting time, for during the 1870s and 1880s French Impressionism was at its height. She had gladly left behind the traditional peasant and toreador pictures of her student years and replaced them with her impressions of modern life. Now, along with

Degas, Monet, Pissarro, and others, Cassatt displayed works of astonishing beauty.

Much of this beauty still went unrecognized. One newspaper reviewer said, "We cannot in fact understand the purpose of the new school.... [The exhibition] was worth seeing for the same reason that one would go to see an exhibition of pictures painted by the lunatics of an insane asylum." So Mary was surprised when she and Degas were mentioned by another writer as "perhaps the only artists who distinguish themselves in this group of Independents." Still another critic appreciated Mary's pictures of women at the theater and at home: "There is nothing more graciously honest and aristocratic than her portraits of young women."

One such "honest and aristocratic" picture was called *A Cup of Tea*, and it was probably shown at the Fifth Impressionist Exhibit, in 1880. This painting offers an insider's view of the world of women in the Cassatts' social circle. In the days before the telephone, women of leisure heard the latest news when they visited each other for afternoon tea. Here, Mary has painted Lydia and a friend relaxing on a plump sofa, taking tea from a silver tea set (which remains in the Cassatt family to this day). The flowered upholstery, striped wallpaper, and gold picture frame give the viewer a glimpse of a beautifully furnished apartment. And the pleasant but formal visit shows a normal afternoon in the Cassatts' orderly life.

Praise from critics made Mary happy, but she also found great satisfaction in the pride of her family. She had worked hard for it. When the Fourth Impressionist Exhibit was over, Mr. Cassatt wrote to Aleck, "She is now known to the Art world as well as to the general public in such a way as not to be forgotten so long as she continues to paint!!"

In 1878 the American artist J. Alden Weir complimented Cassatt on her painting. She responded with her usual modesty: "I thank you very much for all the kind things you say about my work. I only wish I deserved them." Weir wanted Mary to exhibit in New York with the progressive-minded Society of American Artists.

Cassatt badly wanted recognition in her native country and had already sent paintings back to exhibitions at her old school, the Pennsylvania Academy of the Fine Arts. But there were not enough hours in the day for Mary to do everything she wanted to do. In 1878 the French art world was consuming all her time. Regretfully she told Weir, "We [French Impressionists] expect to have our annual exhibition here, and there are so few of us that we are each required to contribute all we have. . . . We are carrying on a despairing fight &

need all our forces." In the same letter, Mary expressed her concern about the future of modern art in America: "I always have a hope that at some future time I shall see New York [as] the [artists'] ground, I think you will create an American school." The following year Mary did manage to send a painting to the Society of American Artists. It was a portrait of her mother, entitled *Reading Le Figaro*.

Mary put her love and understanding of her mother into this portrait, and that is why it is so fine. Katherine Cassatt is shown seated in a comfortable armchair, wearing her glasses and reading the French newspaper. Her quiet strength and calm personality come across clearly. The picture is a subtle blend of curving lines and straight lines, patterned areas and areas of solid color—soft tones of gray, white, and brown. The everyday homeyness of the portrait appealed to one New York reviewer, who wrote, "It is pleasant to see how well an ordinary person dressed in an ordinary way can be made to look." All the Cassatts agreed. They sent the portrait to Aleck, who treasured *Reading Le Figaro* as long as he lived.

As busy as she was with her painting, Mary was soon caught up in another project as well. Degas planned to start an art journal called *Le Jour et La Nuit (Day and Night)*, to be devoted to the medium of prints. He invited Cassatt, Pissarro, Félix Bracquemond, and several others to contribute. "No time to lose!" he said.

Cassatt and Degas were happy to be working together toward the same goal. In artistic matters, they usually saw eye to eye. Mary had become familiar with printmaking during her years at the Pennsylvania Academy of the Fine Arts, and now she threw herself into the work with high hopes.

The engraving method she used was called intaglio, which means "to cut" in Italian. The process was a real challenge. First a drawing was made on a copperplate. Its lines were cut into the plate by hand or else "eaten away"—etched—in an acid bath. Next, ink was rubbed into the cut-away design, and the rest of the plate was wiped clean, Finally the plate, with a sheet of paper on top of it, was rolled through a printing press. This is how the imprint of the drawing was transferred to the paper. Careful artists like Cassatt and Degas printed a plate again and again to achieve the results they wanted.

Degas told Pissarro, "Mlle Cassatt is trying her hand at etching engravings, they are charming." Mary's prints were theater scenes, similar to her oil paintings of elegant women at the Paris Opera House. The subject of Degas's two prints was Mary herself. He depicted her at the Louvre Museum, leaning on her umbrella, gazing at ancient tombs and paintings.

Unfortunately, Degas had an annoying habit of promising more than he could deliver, and he did not produce enough prints in time for publication. *Le Jour et La Nuit* fizzled. Guiltily, Degas explained to Félix Bracquemond, "Impossible for me, with my living to earn, to devote myself entirely to it as yet." Mrs. Cassatt, who seldom lost her temper, was furious that Degas had wasted her daughter's time. "Degas is never ready for anything—This time he has thrown away an excellent chance for all of them," she wrote in a letter to Aleck.

But in Mary's view, no time spent with Degas was wasted. Because he was an artist, he understood her in a way her family never could. And printmaking had brought the two friends even closer. So much of their time was spent alone in front of their easels, that to collaborate on a project was pure pleasure. They gave each other advice and spent whole days in each other's studios.

It was in Degas's studio that Mary learned a new technique for using pastel crayons. He showed her how he sprayed his pastel drawings with steam in order to build up a thick, paste-like texture. He would then work the moistened area with a paintbrush. At various stages in the process, Degas applied a fixative solution, which would preserve the richness of each distinct layer of color.

Mary was quick to see the possibilities. She used Degas's method to create a pastel picture of her sister. Similar to the oil painting of Lydia in pearls, it is called *Lydia Leaning on Her Arms, Seated in a Loge*. Here the pastel colors are not blended smoothly to look like paint but are applied in short, slashing strokes. The result is a study in contrasts, with Lydia's yellow dress as bright as sunshine, her face in bluish shadow. This work shows Mary's marvelous ability to render light and shade—the colored shade of the Impressionists—and it won the admiration of her colleagues in the movement.

In 1880 a joyful family reunion gave Mary a fresh set of models for her paintings. Aleck and his young family came to France for the first of many visits. While he and his wife, Lois, stayed in Paris to shop, their children went to live with their grandparents, Aunt "Liddy," and Aunt Mary.

Mary had rented a country house at Marly-le-Roi for the long, happy summer. There, Eddie, Katharine, Robbie, and Elsie had so much fun that their mother feared they were being spoiled. Their devoted Aunt Mary took them on adventurous outings in her carriage. They went to see the splendid palace and gardens at nearby Versailles. They witnessed a dramatic hot-air balloon launching, and Katharine rode on an elephant.

Perhaps because she had no children of her own, Mary had a special feeling for her nieces and nephews. She was especially fond of Robbie, who showed an early talent for drawing and painting. She bought the children small presents, told them stories, and delighted in their company. And they loved her in return.

The warm months at Marly were a perfect time for Mary Cassatt to be an aunt—and an artist. She kept a treasure chest filled with toys and candy so the rambunctious children would sit still when posing for her. Bribes came in handy at sittings because little Robbie Cassatt "teased his poor Aunt wriggling about like a flea."

But the children sat very still and listened when their grandmother read fairy tales to them. How well Mary captured such moments can be seen in her painting *Mrs. Cassatt Reading to Her Grandchildren*. Although the children and the reader are inside, the scene has a fresh, open-air feeling. Mary used dashes of red and blue, soft greens and browns, and plenty of white to show the effects of hazy sunlight streaming through the window.

The family became so attached to this peaceful picture that they would not permit Mary to sell it. "She could hardly sell her mother and nieces & nephew I think," wrote Mrs. Cassatt. And after the children had returned to America, their grandfather stared longingly at the painting. He wrote to the children, "It makes me wish often and often that I could hear your little voices call as I heard them when the picture was being painted."

It was a productive summer. Mary did an oil painting of Lydia crocheting in the green garden. She did a colorful pastel of her five-year-old niece, called *Elsie in a Blue Chair,* and painted *Mother About to Wash Her Sleepy Child,* the first of many mother-and-child pictures to come. And though she was not to be satisfied with the results, Mary began a portrait of her brother Aleck.

While Aleck posed, brother and sister had precious time to talk. Although he was shy outside the family circle, Aleck had become extremely successful in business. As vice president of the Pennsylvania Railroad, he was one of the richest men in America. (He was to become president of the railroad in 1899.) And true to Cassatt tradition, Aleck was loyal—and generous—to those he loved. In 1879 he had bought his parents a carriage and a pony named Bichette. In the same year, he set up a trust fund for them. Now Aleck was happy to be near Mary, whom he adored as much as ever.

He and Mary talked about old times and about the family passion—horses. Mary had painted several pictures of family members on horseback. She was almost as softhearted with the Cassatts' horses as she was with the children, always making sure that the animals were treated kindly. For his part, Aleck owned racehorses. One of them, The Bard, was to become famous after winning the Preakness race in 1886.

Mary skillfully led their conversations from real horses to the horse-race pictures of Edgar Degas. She explained Degas's genius to Aleck as she had to Louisine Elder in 1875. It was Mary's strong desire that Aleck should own some of her friend's unique work.

In fact, one of Mary Cassatt's lifelong missions was to encourage people to buy French Impressionist paintings. Long before it became fashionable, Mary had bought some for herself with the small profits from the sale of her own pictures. Always unselfish in promoting the work of other artists, she had a keen eye for quality and total confidence in her own taste.

Aleck knew a lot about railroads, not art. He trusted his sister's judgment and was willing to let Mary choose paintings for him. Still, she liked to show him photographs of the works in question: "I don't like to buy anything for you without your having some idea of what it would be like."

Always demanding the lowest prices possible, Cassatt selected for her brother some landscapes by Monet, one by Pissarro, two by Renoir, Morisot's

River Scene, and, of course, works by Degas. (Pictures by Cassatt were always free for Aleck!) When Aleck returned to Philadelphia, Robert Cassatt wrote to him about a Degas and a Pissarro that Mary had chosen: "When you get these pictures you will probably be the only person in Philadelphia who owns specimens of either of the masters—Mame's friends the Elders [Louisine's parents in New York] have a Degas & a Pissarro & Mame thinks that there are no others in America."

Mame was right. There were no other paintings in America by the great Impressionists. The collections that she began for Alexander Cassatt and Louisine Elder Havemeyer were the first of their kind in Mary's native land.

However, Lois Cassatt thought buying pictures was a waste of money. And she was jealous of the time that her husband spent with his talented sister. ("The sitting business is a nuisance," she complained.) The problem was that the two women were about as different as two people could be. Lois was a disapproving sort of person, while Mary was forceful and sure of herself in a way that Lois could not understand. In a letter to her sister Harriet, Lois confided, "I cannot abide Mary and never will. I cannot tell why but there is something utterly obnoxious about that girl. . . . She is too self-important and I can't put up with it. . . . She tries to be polite to me however, and so we get on well enough. The children all seem to prefer her to the others, strange to say." Lois was the only Cassatt who was not sad to say good-bye when her family returned to America in the fall.

When they were separated from each other, the Cassatts consoled themselves by sending presents. As Christmas drew near, Mary mailed a big box full of gifts to her nieces and nephews. Eager to encourage Robbie's interest in art, Mary sent him a paint box. She advised him, "to draw very carefully a portrait . . . beginning with the eyes (remember) & send it to Grandmother, that would please her more than any other Christmas present she could get."

The Paris Cassatts missed American food, so Aleck's gift to them was a crate filled with mouthwatering treats: turkeys, hams, ducks, cranberries, sweet potatoes, apples, and even oysters. The recipients relished every bite.

During the winter of 1881, Mary put the finishing touches on the pictures she had painted at Marly. When Degas saw them, he said, "What [Mary] did in the country looks very well in studio light. It is much more firm and noble than what she did last year." The paintings were ready to be shown at the Sixth Impressionist Exhibit, in the spring of 1881. For Mary Cassatt, the show was a smashing success. It brought her sales—and real fame.

Art buyers and critics alike were enchanted by Cassatt's sunlit gardens and cozy family groups. "This is family life painted with distinction and love," said the writer and critic J. K. Huysmans. He admired the "happy contentment, the quiet friendliness" of Mary's pictures. To Huysmans, Cassatt's children looked real—not sugary sweet as children did in so many other works. The critic went on to say that the Marly paintings established Cassatt as an original artist, "an artist who owes nothing any longer to anyone."

The whole family was overjoyed with Mary's rave reviews and excellent sales. Yet Mary herself knew that critics and the public alike were fickle. What pleased her more was the fact that artists whom she respected now saw her as their equal and were seeking her out. All the attention was flattering, but Cassatt was a serious and private person. She was too levelheaded to be carried away by the sweet taste of success. "Too much pudding," she exclaimed, and hurried back to her paints.

Chapter Seven

Family Cares

Soon Mary's happiness with her career was overshadowed by family grief. Lydia Cassatt had begun to lose her battle with kidney disease. Mary wrote to Aleck, "It was on Tuesday that the worst attack came. She lay with her eyes wide open and totally blind, and remained so for twenty-four hours. Of course, it seemed to us the end. . . . However, this time it was not so."

The doctors told Mary that Lydia was dying. She dropped everything to nurse her sister. And because Mrs. Cassatt had a heart condition, Mary insisted that "Mother must not be allowed to do anything." Exhausted by days and nights at Lydia's bedside, Mary wrote again to Aleck, "Give my love to all and excuse this letter but I am so tired I can hardly hold a pen." Robert Cassatt also sent news to Philadelphia: "Lydia says [Mary] has developed

Plate 1: LITTLE GIRL IN A BLUE ARMCHAIR
1878 oil on canvas

National Gallery of Art

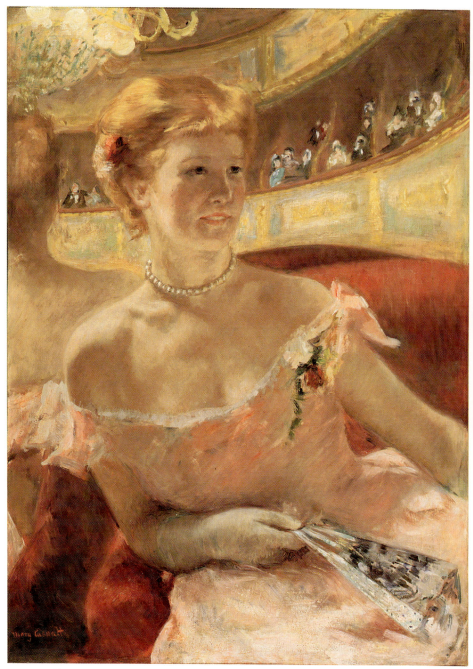

Plate 2: LYDIA IN A LOGE, WEARING A PEARL NECKLACE
1879   *oil on canvas*

Plate 3: READING LE FIGARO
c.1878   oil on canvas

Plate 4: MRS. CASSATT READING TO HER GRANDCHILDREN
1880   oil on canvas

Plate 5: LYDIA WORKING AT A TAPESTRY FRAME
1881, oil on canvas
Flint Institute of Arts

Plate 6: LITTLE GIRL IN A BIG STRAW HAT
c.1886 oil on canvas

Plate 7: WOMAN BATHING
c.1891   *color print with drypoint and soft-ground etching*

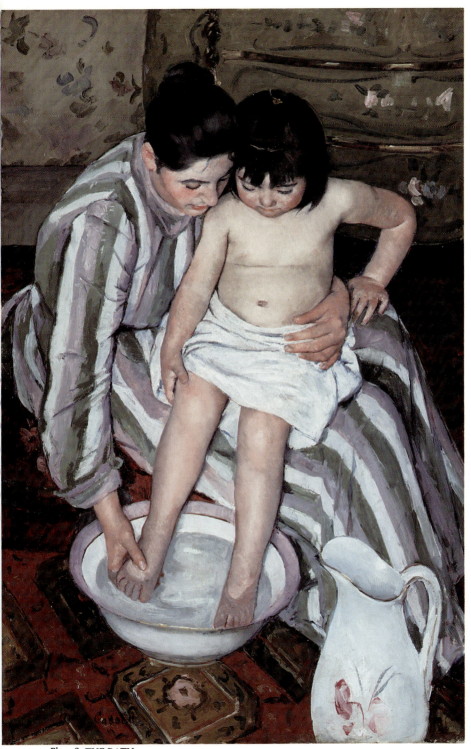
Plate 8: THE BATH
1891-92   oil on canvas

Plate 9: CHILD WITH RED HAT
  c.1901   pastel

into a most excellent nurse.—As far as her art is concerned the summer has been lost to her." It was a sacrifice that Mary made willingly.

On November 7, 1882, Lydia died. As she had requested, she was buried in the Marly countryside. Mary Cassatt was overwhelmed by sadness. She had lost the companion of a lifetime—kind and gentle Lydia, with whom she had planned to spend her old age. Mary could not bring herself to work at all for several months.

Yet she had created a lasting tribute to her beloved sister in so many paintings. There was Lydia at the theater or crocheting in the garden, Lydia reading or driving a carriage or drinking her tea.

Lydia Working at a Tapestry Frame glows with soft daylight. It is fitting that this is Mary's last picture of her favorite model. While Impressionist techniques (visible brushwork and blurred outlines) were used for the background, Lydia's head is depicted in a more classical manner. The details of her pale face, as she bends over her weaving, are lovingly and precisely shown. It is almost as if Mary wanted to fix Lydia's features forever in her memory.

Aleck's family came to Paris immediately after Lydia's death, and their presence consoled Mary a bit. In her grief, she even reached out to Lois, who wrote to her mother, "Mary seems to be most anxious to be friendly and proposes something for us to do together every day." Cassatt had told Lois that she feared facing old age without a family of her own: "[Mary] is very lonesome . . . and says she feels now that perhaps she would have been better off to have married when she thinks of being left alone in the world."

But gradually, Mary's natural optimism and interest in life returned. She needed to be busy. Her brother Gardner had recently married, and Mary sent a gift of pearls to his wife, Jennie. She also sent presents to her old friend Louisine Elder, who had married Henry O. Havemeyer, the millionaire "king" of the sugar refining industry. Mary went shopping with Lois and bought stylish dresses at the exclusive fashion houses of Paris. She began work on another portrait of Aleck. And she became the firm friend and ally of her nephew Eddie, who stayed in Paris to go to school after the rest of his family sailed back to Philadelphia.

Fourteen-year-old Eddie was deeply homesick at first and had trouble adjusting to the foreign school. Mr. Cassatt noticed that Eddie "had to put up with an immense amount of hazing and nagging from the boys" until he learned to defend himself. Aunt Mary took him under her wing. Her sensitivity toward young people is evident in a letter she wrote to Aleck about his son: "I hope [Eddie] won't feel too lonely. I wonder if Lois won't reconsider her orders not to let him play cricket on Sunday afternoon, tell her I am afraid he will be very dull with only us to talk to."

Mary made sure that Eddie took horseback riding lessons until he became as skilled as all the adult Cassatts were. She took him to see the thrilling horse race, the Grand Prix, and the two of them came home "looking like millers actually white with dust" from the track. Humorously, Eddie described to his mother Mary's plans to do his portrait: "Aunt Mary is going to paint a water color picture of me about a foot square. My head is to be about an inch and a half in diameter so you can imagine how small it is to be."

His aunt's support helped Eddie to thrive. He became one of the school's best students, graduating third in his class, with high honors and prizes. But Mary knew that his success had not come easily. She wrote to his father, "Poor child it has been like a penitentiary to him . . . no one knew what he had suffered at that school although he felt that it had done him good."

Life was not easy for the Impressionists, either. In 1882 a stock market crash in France dried up their already small pool of buyers. Their faithful dealer, Paul Durand-Ruel, was nearly bankrupt. In a generous effort to help, Mary Cassatt lent money to Durand-Ruel. She also introduced him to several wealthy Americans in the hope that they would buy his Impressionist paintings. But what the painter Cézanne had said about the Impressionists in 1877 still held true: "Streams of gold are not exactly flowing into their pocket[s]."

Monet and Renoir had grown weary of walking from door to door, peddling their paintings. In their struggle to avoid starvation, they were returning from time to time to the Salon to exhibit. Renoir was practical about this decision: "There are scarcely 15 art collectors in Paris capable of liking a painter without the backing of the Salon. . . . Unfortunately I have one goal in life, and that is to increase the value of my canvases." In addition to sales, Renoir wanted recognition: "The painting of an unknown or little-known man is lost forever."

Of course, Cassatt and Degas were upset at this blow to Impressionist unity. They had taken seriously their vow never to return to the Salon. And although their work was now selling better than that of Monet or Renoir, they, too, had risked being unknown forever. "Do I care a jot about the public?" Degas would one day shout.

To make matters worse, the Impressionists were arguing violently over the issue of membership in their movement. Many of them wanted to keep standards high by restricting the group to painters of Impressionist technique only. In his usual forceful way, Degas disagreed. He was in favor of including any excellent artist—regardless of style—who would pledge independence from the Salon. A more varied membership might also increase sales, he reasoned.

There were shouting matches. Bitter letters were exchanged. The Impressionist painter Gustave Caillebotte wrote to Pissarro about Degas, "This man has gone sour. He doesn't hold the big place he ought according to his talent and, although he will never admit it, he bears the whole world a grudge." The wise and practical Camille Pissarro tried to keep peace among the Impressionists. But Degas was not one to compromise. He boycotted the Seventh Impressionist Exhibit of 1882. Out of loyalty, Mary Cassatt withdrew as well.

The troubles of 1882—Lydia's death and the Impressionist boycott—slowed Mary down a great deal. But they didn't stop her. Her art was actually reaching a turning point. Mary had begun to move away from pure Impressionism, where light and color were just as important as the subject itself. She was becoming more interested in crisp, clear line. *Lady at the Tea Table*, painted in 1883, is an example of Mary's change to a more structured, linear approach.

The subject of the painting is Mrs. Robert Moore Riddle, who was a first cousin of Katherine Cassatt. Mary and her mother had visited Mrs. Riddle and her daughter, Annie Scott, in London. After the visit, Mrs. Riddle surprised Mary with a gift—a "most lovely old Japanese tea & coffee set" made of porcelain.

To repay her relative's kindness, Mary Cassatt painted her portrait. It was a remarkable one. Mrs. Riddle, whose face and bearing look rather stern, seems to be absorbed in her own thoughts. She is seated behind the Japanese porcelain; its purplish blue is highlighted by the darker blue of Mrs. Riddle's dress. Touches of white lace accentuate the shades of blue. Because the form of every object stands out boldly, the picture is a departure from strict Impressionism. Every outline is sharply drawn.

Mrs. Riddle didn't care about Mary's changing style, though. She only wondered, why had Mary painted her nose so big? After all, she thought, the purpose of a portrait was to create an exact likeness of a person. Mrs. Riddle was thoroughly insulted and refused to take the picture home. Mary, in turn, was appalled at the woman's ingratitude. But Mrs. Cassatt, who knew her relatives well, had predicted trouble. In a letter to Aleck, she had written, "They are not very artistic in their

Mrs. Riddle, the subject of Lady at the Tea Table, was not pleased with her portrait.

likes & dislikes of pictures & as a likeness is a hard thing to make to please the nearest friends I don't know what the result will be." The result was that Mary hid *Lady at the Tea Table* in a closet, where it would spend the next thirty-one years. "I felt I never wanted to see it again," commented the artist years later.

Not everyone thought the portrait was a failure. Degas called it "distinction itself." He appreciated Cassatt's emphasis on the well-drawn line rather than on flowing color and splashy brushwork. Degas had always worshiped the neat, classical style of Ingres and had deprived himself of necessities so that he could buy pictures by the great French artist. As a young man, Degas had met Ingres and had taken to heart the master's advice: "Study lines, young man. Draw lots of lines, either from memory or from nature."

And the mature Degas said, "The dancer is for me only an excuse to draw." While the other Impressionists were captivated by light and color, Degas concentrated on the underlying structure of things. He preferred to paint the graceful shape of a ballerina's leg instead of dappled sunlight on water. In fact, Degas had once looked at a Monet seascape and quipped, "I'm leaving. All these reflections on the water hurt my eyes."

Mary Cassatt's latest work revealed her own

love of line and form. Once more, the two artists found that they had much in common. Their taste set them apart from the other Impressionists in the movement. They really were what they had always wanted to be called—Independents.

But when Degas painted Mary's portrait, it was her turn to be insulted. She said of the picture, "It has qualities of art, but it is so distressing and shows me as a person so repugnant that I would not want anyone to know that I posed for it." Degas had painted her in a brown dress and ribboned hat, leaning forward in her chair. Mary, who had never been happy with her looks, was not flattered by the image of her pointed chin, her large hands, her almost masculine pose. Fortunately, Degas had seen the inner characteristics of his friend, too. The portrait conveys Mary's intelligence, her confidence, and her strength.

She had to be strong. Her mother's heart condition was getting worse, and Mrs. Cassatt was often so stiff with rheumatism that she could barely walk. Once again, care of the sick fell to Mary. On doctor's orders, she took her mother to the milder climate of Spain. A letter to Aleck shows that Mary, too, was suffering: "My poor painting is sadly interrupted, I have no time now for anything & the constant anxiety takes all heart out of me; my only hope is that this change will set

Mother right for a time."

And back in Paris, Mr. Cassatt was as stubborn as he had ever been. He had set his mind against moving, although his wife's doctor had forbidden her to climb stairs and advised her to find an apartment with an elevator. Mary couldn't budge her father. She pleaded for Aleck's help: "[Father] really cannot be made to understand that Mother is a sick woman. . . . The fact is that apartment is too much for her, those five flights of stairs; Father does not feel them and thinks nobody else ought to." Robert Cassatt did not like taking instruction from women. Only after a strongly worded message from Aleck did he sign the lease for 14, rue Pierre Charron.

Mary quickly chose lace curtains, fringed lamp shades, and other furnishings for the new place. With the help of her German housekeeper, Mathilde Vallet ("Taudy"), she coped with the details of moving. At the same time, Cassatt kept a watchful eye on her mother's slow recovery and tried to help her father adjust to their new home. Worn out, Mary wrote, "Father went on like a crazy man for the first three weeks and nearly killed me."

The new apartment, complete with elevator, was larger and more convenient than the old one. But there was still much to be done before it would feel like home. In order to write to Lois, the artist had to "seize a moment from housekeeping, painting & oyster frying." It seems a miracle that Mary managed to squeeze in any painting at all.

"I am at work again," reported Cassatt in 1885. What a relief it must have been! She made peace with her father and completed a pastel of him sitting on his favorite mare, Isabelle. Mary gave the picture to Gard and told Aleck of their father's satisfaction with it: "He is much delighted, but he says you will never believe that [the horse] is as handsome as I have made her."

At this time also, Mary painted two oils of children that perfectly capture the subjects' moods. *The Sisters* is a loosely brushed, sketchlike painting in which two little girls sit with their arms around each other. The sisters' expressive brown eyes are the focal point of the picture. They gaze upward from the canvas with a look that seems part wonder, part worry.

By contrast, *Two Children at the Seashore* projects the fun of a day at the beach, where two small girls are digging in the sand. Here Mary has worked special magic, because the little models seem unposed, totally unaware that an adult is watching—and painting—them. The background of sea and sailboats is done with Impressionist softness, while Cassatt used her new method of firmer modeling to shape the children's rounded bodies.

Mary was working with renewed zest because the Impressionists were planning another exhibit, the first to be held in four years. Pissarro visited her to discuss which artists should be included. But the Impressionists were bickering now more than they had in 1882, the year of Degas's and Cassatt's boycott. In a group of such strong-minded individuals, any issue was fair game for a fight—even the issue of setting a date for the show.

Degas wanted to schedule the exhibit for the same time as the Salon show, from May 15 to June 15, 1886. Others felt that fierce competition from the Salon would hurt Impressionist sales. Pissarro noted bitterly that Mary Cassatt encouraged so many people to buy Degas's work that perhaps Degas didn't really need to sell more. He wrote to his son Lucien, "Degas doesn't care, he doesn't have to sell, he will always have Mlle Cassatt." Pissarro added that it was easy not to care about money "when you don't have to wonder where your next meal will come from!"

It is true that neither Cassatt nor Degas had to worry from one meal to the next. Cassatt, especially, lived comfortably from the sale of her paintings, whereas the works of Pissarro, now priceless museum treasures, were largely ignored during his lifetime.

But Mary was rich only compared with some of

her desperately poor colleagues. She resented their false notion that she could rely on a family fortune. Robert Cassatt lived on a small retirement income, supplemented by financial help from his sons, Aleck and Gard. Mary used the profits from her work to buy clothes, to care for her horse, and to support her studio. Because she lived with her parents, she had few other expenses. She was able to save a good deal of money over the years.

Cassatt was generous with her savings. She joined Degas and Morisot in paying all the costs of the upcoming exhibit. She was to receive a share of the profits—although, Mr. Cassatt observed, "Needless to say they do not hope for or expect any." Because he was helping with the finances, Degas was permitted his choice of the date. With Monet and Renoir refusing to participate, the show opened on May 15, in rooms above a restaurant at 1, rue Lafitte.

It was the Eighth Impressionist Exhibit, and it was to be the last. It had become too difficult to hold together a unified movement. While the artists all saw themselves as painters of modern life, they had branched out into a variety of styles. It was in their nature to experiment. In the 1860s and 1870s the Impressionists had rebelled against tradition, and their ideas were still growing, still changing. Pissarro wrote of "the totally different future that is being prepared."

It was Pissarro who invited two newcomers, Georges Seurat and Paul Signac, to take part in the show. Their work was so controversial that they were forced to hang their pictures in a separate room. Seurat's large painting, *Sunday Afternoon on the Island of La Grande Jatte* attracted much attention and—as is often the case with something new—scorn. The young man had invented a style of brushwork called *pointillism*, which consisted of thousands of tiny dots. This highly organized method of painting came to be labeled Neo-Impressionism, and it was a decisive break with the recent Impressionist past.

Mary Cassatt's own past and future were represented at the 1886 exhibit. One of the six oil paintings she displayed was *Susan on a Balcony Holding a Dog*. Painted during her early Impressionist years, it is a lovely, sunlit view of a young woman holding Mary's dog Batty in her lap. Cassatt's recent move toward strong line could be seen in another entry, called *Girl Arranging Her Hair*.

Mary had painted *Girl Arranging Her Hair* while she was angry with Degas. In one of his mysterious negative moods, he had implied that women—Mary included—knew nothing about style in art. To prove him wrong, Mary deliberately chose a model who was not at all attractive. Yet through fine drawing and design, she created a very appealing picture, indeed. Cassatt got the last laugh, because when Degas saw *Girl Arranging Her Hair*, he wrote to her, exclaiming, "What drawing! What style!" He bought the painting immediately and kept it all his life.

During the planning of the Eighth Impressionist Exhibit, Durand-Ruel had seen how hard it would be to organize any more such collections. He started to focus on individual shows for the artists. But his rival, the art dealer Georges Petit, had also begun to sell Impressionist work, and Durand-Ruel faced serious competition. He came up with a new plan: He would bring Impressionism to the United States.

Mary Cassatt jumped at the chance to educate the people of her own country. She wrote Aleck and the Havemeyers, asking them to lend some of their French Impressionist works to Durand-Ruel for the exhibit. She also asked them to tell their friends about the event, for Mary hoped to excite the curiosity of as many Americans as possible.

America's first major Impressionist exhibit opened on April 10, 1886, at the American Art Association, in New York. Durand-Ruel had brought with him giant crates filled with pictures. There were seventeen works by Manet, twenty-three by Degas, forty-eight Monets, thirty-eight

Renoirs, forty-two Pissarros, and several paintings by Sisley and Morisot. Because she had been so busy with family cares, Cassatt contributed only two pictures. But they were superb ones—the portrait of her mother called *Reading Le Figaro* and the picture *Mrs. Cassatt Reading to Her Grandchildren.*

Reactions were mixed, but the American public was surprisingly respectful. The *New York Daily Tribune* published an article about the new "interesting movement in foreign art." Perhaps because they had no centuries-old art tradition themselves, the Americans were more open-minded than the French had been. Durand-Ruel felt welcomed and wrote, "Don't think that the Americans are savages. On the contrary, they are less ignorant, less bound by routine, than our French collectors." Renoir, too, was happy with the American public: "It doesn't think it necessary to sneer at things it doesn't understand."

Sales from the exhibition totaled $18,000. Mary Cassatt was much encouraged. She knew that the paintings bought by Americans would in time be donated to museums. And it was her fervent wish that American museums would one day be as filled with masterpieces as those in Europe.

After the Impressionist exhibits in Paris and New York, Mary turned her attention to her family. The Cassatts celebrated the birth of Gard's first child, Gardner, Jr. And in 1887, Mary and her parents moved—again—to 10, rue de Marignan, a roomier apartment conveniently close to the center of Paris.

The apartment was sunny, with high ceilings and central heating. It was perfect for Mary because it had room for a studio, and she was to keep it all her life. This time, to everyone's relief, Robert Cassatt had approved of the change. He admitted to Aleck that he had taken the move "rather pleasantly in fact."

More pleasant news came as the family followed Aleck's amazing luck at the racetrack. Cassatts in France and America read every bit of racing news as Aleck's horse The Bard galloped to one victory after another. Mrs. Cassatt claimed that she didn't approve of horse racing, but even she snatched the paper as soon as it arrived. In her dry way, Mary joked about her brother's hobby: "He's corrupting all the old ladies in the family."

As the decade drew to a close, there was bad luck, too. In the summer of 1888, Mary went riding with her father in the Bois de Boulogne and fell from her horse. Suffering a broken right leg and a dislocated left shoulder, Cassatt was told that she could never ride again. This was deeply disappointing. Degas, who understood how Mary felt about being "deprived . . . of her horsewoman's passion," brought her a bouquet of flowers. It was a particularly touching gesture, because Degas believed that flowers should never be removed from the garden. (He had once thrown a friend's bouquet out of a window in protest!)

While Mary waited for her leg to heal, did she look back over the years to see how far she had come? What had once been a young girl's faraway dream had become a reality. Full of hope, Mary had sailed to Europe to learn everything she could about art. In the spirited company of the French Impressionists, her talent had unfolded. Now, at the age of forty-four, Cassatt was a mature artist who had mastered color, line, form, and composition. Even as she left behind her purely Impressionist style, Mary Cassatt remained an Impressionist at heart. For she found inspiration in her own life and times. And she believed that an artist should be free to paint without fearing the opinion of a jury—one of whose members might even be a pharmacist!

Chapter Eight

Japanese Prints and a Chicago Mural

Paris in the 1890s was a whirlwind of activity, a place of lightning-fast change. It was the beginning of the Belle Époque (Beautiful Epoch), those two hopeful decades before the horror of World War I. France's economic slump lifted as industry and trade expanded worldwide. A lucky few made vast fortunes, while millions in the growing middle class could afford a better life than ever before. Poor factory workers—and their children—labored such long hours that they seldom saw the sun, but even they had some hope for the future. For it was an age of discovery. Amazing new inventions gave Parisians a belief in progress and in the century soon to come.

Signs of the future were exciting and sometimes frightening. They were popping up everywhere. People marveled at the latest gadgets—

phonographs and hand-held cameras, typewriters and telephones. They even viewed the magic of the first silent films. The newly built Eiffel Tower lit the night with an electric beam, so much more dazzling than yesterday's mellow gaslight. And in the 1890s, the golden age of the bicycle began rolling slowly to an end. People stared, horses reared, as the first automobiles whizzed by at the unheard of speed of fifteen miles an hour!

Parisians clamored for entertainment and novelty. They idolized the actress "The Divine Sarah" Bernhardt. They ate, drank, and applauded the singers at the city's many café concerts. Aristocrats and workers alike caroused at the Moulin Rouge, a dance hall with as many sideshows as a circus.

Mary Cassatt was much too respectable to take part in a wild nightlife. Nor was she interested in one. She was, of course, passionately interested in the art of her day. People now had more money to spend on paintings, and a rich variety of styles began to fill the galleries. One could still find the Salon art of the academic establishment. And there was Impressionism, which had opened the door to Neo-Impressionism. Newer on the scene were the symbolic paintings of Paul Gauguin and the flamboyant poster art of Henri de Toulouse-Lautrec.

With no more Impressionist exhibits to prepare for, Cassatt was on her own. She was sensitive to all the currents running through the art world and was not content to stay in a rut. But where would fresh inspiration come from? It came from halfway across the world, when Mary saw the delicate and beautiful art of Japan.

Parisians had been charmed for decades by Japanese culture. Kimonos, blue-and-white porcelain, fans, and Japanese prints sold well in the city. So when the École des Beaux-Arts held an exhibit of hundreds of Japanese woodblock prints from the eighteenth and nineteenth centuries, it was a big success. Cassatt and her friends were spellbound. The French Impressionists felt a special kinship with the Japanese artists. Both groups loved to use bright blocks of color, cropped composition, flattened *perspective* (a technique used to give the appearance of depth), and scenes from everyday life. Pissarro reflected the opinion of many of his friends when he called the Japanese artists the original "marvellous Impressionist[s]."

Mary Cassatt visited the show again and again. She told Berthe Morisot, "You couldn't dream of anything more beautiful. I dream of it and don't think of anything else." Soon landscape prints by Hiroshige and figures by Utamaro decorated Mary's apartment walls. She admired her purchases—and studied them. Attracted to the pared-down simplicity of the prints, Cassatt made a decision. She, too, would learn to draw without a single unnecessary line.

But how could Mary adapt Japanese ideas to her own vision? How could she adapt Japanese technique? The Japanese made their prints by carving on a block of wood and printing the raised design that resulted. Mary, on the other hand, was skilled in the European method of intaglio, in which the drawing is cut into a copperplate. After much practice, she found a way to blend the spirit of the Japanese prints with her own intaglio method.

Printing required infinite patience and whole days and evenings in the studio, where she had her own printing press. But Mary was a perfectionist: "There are two ways for a painter, the broad and easy one or the narrow and hard one." She often combined three intricate types of intaglio to create one print: drypoint, soft-ground etching, and aquatint.

In drypoint, the drawing is cut directly onto the plate with a sharp needle. Since one false move can ruin the whole plate, there is no room for mistakes. Mary welcomed the drawing practice this technique gave her, saying, "In drypoint you are down to the bare bones, you can't cheat."

She could make a fuzzier line with soft-ground etching. Here the plate is covered with a layer of acid-resistant wax and a piece of paper placed on top. When Mary drew on the paper, the wax directly underneath was lifted off, and the exposed lines could be etched in acid.

Aquatint is the third type of intaglio. Mary used this method to create shaded areas on a print, rather than lines. First she dusted parts of the plate with acid-resistant grains of rosin, which stuck to the plate when heated. Then she dipped the plate in acid, which would eat into the metal surrounding the tiny grains. The result, when printed, was faintly speckled shading.

Cassatt learned to color her prints with as much finesse as Hiroshige or Utamaro. While Europeans applied their colors *after* the printing process, Mary favored the Japanese way and was one of the first Westerners to try it. She hand-rubbed her colors onto the design *before* the final printing. Her skill with color became the envy of her French colleagues. Pissarro wrote to his son about the "rare and exquisite" effects that he saw in Cassatt's studio: "adorable blues, fresh rose . . . The result is admirable, as beautiful as Japanese work, and it's done with printer's ink!"

Mary had expected to show a set of ten stunning color prints as a member of the Society of Painters-Printmakers—a group composed of some of her friends from Impressionist days. But for some unknown reason, her colleagues suddenly became "patriotic." They added the word *French* to the society's name and kicked out American-born Mary Cassatt and West Indies–born Camille Pissarro. Mary left a dinner meeting of the society almost in tears.

But this rejection was a blessing in disguise. Durand-Ruel arranged for Pissarro and Cassatt to have their own exhibits in his gallery, right next to the society's display. At forty-six, Mary was to have her first—and long overdue—one-woman show. Her loyal friend Pissarro suspected that the "patriots" would be jealous, because their prints were "ugly, heavy, lusterless, and commercial" compared with Cassatt's.

Jealous—and awed—they were. When Degas saw the print *Woman Bathing*, he was moved to exclaim, "I am not willing to admit that a woman can draw that well." Mary Cassatt had achieved simplicity. She had learned what to leave out, as well as what to put in. With one "floating line" she could suggest a woman's curved back, a baby's fat cheek, a mother's tight hug. Some of the most eye-catching prints, like *The Letter*, contained an added twist: The artist had acknowledged her debt to the Japanese by giving her models Asian facial features.

Cassatt's contribution to the field of graphics (drawing and printing) was original—an extraordinary meeting of the art of East and West. In France she was now well known as a printmaker. Her first solo show had done wonders for her spirits and her pocketbook. Now Durand-Ruel decided that the time was right to take the prints to America.

Mary had already sent some earlier prints to Samuel Avery, president of the Board of Trustees of New York's Metropolitan Museum of Art. She wrote to tell him of the upcoming show: "I am very anxious to know what you think of these new etchings. It amused me very much to do them although it was hard work." She promised to donate a painting to the Metropolitan Museum if New Yorkers showed interest in her work. And her success in Paris gave her every reason to believe that they would. As Mrs. Cassatt observed, Mary was now "intent on fame and money . . . and counts on her fellow country men now that she has made a reputation here [in France]."

It was not to be. In New York, not one print was sold. The negative response helped fuel Mary's feelings of neglect by her native land. She wrote sadly to Durand-Ruel's son Joseph: "I am very glad you have any sale for them in Paris. Of course it is more flattering from an Art point of view than if they sold in America, but I am still very much disappointed that my compatriotes have so little liking for any of my work."

The Letter, *printed on a copperplate, was displayed at Mary's first one-woman show.*

Mary's sadness over the failure of the New York show was slight, however, compared with her grief over the death of her father. Robert Cassatt had been feeling ill since the summer of 1891, but his death in December of that year came as a surprise. While Mary was relieved that her father had not suffered much at the end, she wrote to Aleck, "I am very much depressed in every way and long for a change."

Change came in the form of a new project, another attempt to gain artistic recognition in America. This time the dynamic Bertha Palmer, star of Chicago society, was involved. Chicago leaders were planning a gala celebration of American life, to be called the World's Columbian Exposition. Mrs. Palmer was looking for female artists to decorate the walls of the Woman's Building, which would be dedicated to the lives and accomplishments of women. She asked the Connecticut-born artist Mary Fairchild MacMonnies to paint a mural to be called *Primitive Woman*. *Modern Woman* was the topic offered to Mary Cassatt.

Mary couldn't resist the chance to try again, and she said yes to Mrs. Palmer. But she did have doubts about accepting the commission. She told her friend Louisine, "At first I was horrified, but gradually I began to think it would be great fun to do something I had never done before." Her first work of public art—displayed at a world's fair—might finally establish Cassatt's reputation in America. And the theme "Modern Woman" was dear to her heart. At a time when women could not vote, when their role in society was strictly limited,

Mary wanted to have her say. She herself was living proof of what a determined woman could do.

She began work in a specially built glass-roofed studio in the country, at Château Bachivillers. A trench was dug into the studio floor so that Mary wouldn't need a ladder. She could reach the top of her canvas by simply lowering it into the trench. She explained to Bertha Palmer that her idea was to paint a decorative mural "as bright, as gay, as amusing as possible." It would be similar to an old tapestry, "brilliant yet soft."

The pressure was intense. There was much to plan and much to do. "I am afraid my work will show signs of hurry," wrote Mary. She had only six months to fill an enormous canvas; she could have used two years. Frustrated at times, she craved advice from her mentor Degas. But Degas had angrily opposed the project from the start, so Mary could not speak to him about it: "If he happens to be in the mood he would demolish me so completely that I could never pick myself up in time to finish."

Along the way, there were mix-ups over which the efficient Mrs. Palmer had no control. Mary told her, "I hardly think women could be more unbusinesslike than some of the men are." Letters flew back and forth between Paris and Chicago. "Contract received, conditions impossible . . ."

wrote Cassatt at one point. She refused to submit a preliminary sketch, and she did not want to wait until completion of the project to receive her $3,000 fee. Her sarcastic comment to her fellow mural painter, Mary MacMonnies, was that "certainly Chicago seems to reserve endless surprises for us."

With Mrs. Palmer's help, the "endless surprises" were ironed out. And Mary finished her canvas—all 58 x 12 feet of it—in time for the great Chicago fair. The mural was Mary Cassatt's statement of women's rights, her forward-looking view of women's potential.

Modern Woman was indeed unlike anything Mary had tried before. Its three sections were painted in rich, jewel-like tones of blues and greens. The entire mural was edged with a wide border strewn with flowers and babies. The border itself was rimmed by a band of gold. Each panel symbolized an important aspect of a modern woman's life.

"Young Women Plucking the Fruits of Knowledge or Science" is the central and largest panel. The young women in the orchard, dressed in the latest fashion, are picking fruit. They are hungry—not for apples, but for the "knowledge or science" that the fruit symbolizes. In the left-hand panel, "Young Girls Pursuing Fame," a group of girls

Modern Woman, 58 x 12 feet—Mary's tribute to womanhood

is being chased by a gaggle of geese. (Might the geese symbolize foolish conformity?) And the right-hand panel, "Arts, Music, Dancing," stresses women's valuable role in these disciplines.

A male friend complained to Mary that there were no men in her mural. Weren't men also a part of women's lives? he wondered. Cassatt replied tartly, "Men, I have no doubt, are painted in all their vigor on the walls of other buildings; to us the sweetness of childhood, the charm of womanhood; if I have not conveyed some sense of that charm . . . if I have not been absolutely feminine, then I have failed."

Twenty-one million people attended the 1893 World's Columbian Exposition. They saw belly dancers from Egypt, a 264-foot-high Ferris wheel, and a display of inventions that included the first dishwasher. But Mary Cassatt's mural did not attract much attention. It had been placed just under the ceiling of the enormous Woman's Building—so high that it was hard to see. Mary had predicted to Mrs. Palmer that her mural would be ignored "when it is dragged up 48 feet & you will have to stretch your neck to get sight of it all."

Remembering New York's failure to appreciate the color prints, Cassatt was doubly discouraged.

The gap between Mary's reputation in France and in America was made even plainer shortly after the Chicago fair. The French government honored Mary by asking her to donate one of her paintings to the country's modern art collection, housed in the Palais du Luxembourg, in Paris. She wrote to a friend, "After all give me France—women do not have to fight for recognition here, if they do serious work." In the same letter, Mary expressed her admiration for Bertha Palmer: "I suppose it is Mrs. Palmer's French blood which gives her . . . her determination that women should be *someone* and not *something*."

After the Chicago disappointment, a rest in the south of France at Cap d'Antibes did Mary good. She and her mother were joined there by Gardner and his family. Now Mary had another wriggling, impatient little nephew to distract her.

One day, five-year-old Gardner Cassatt was posing for his portrait, *Boy in the Sailor Suit*. He was overcome by boredom and spat in Aunt Mary's face. His outraged mother locked him in a closet for punishment. But Mary, more than most people, understood frustration. She rode into town, bought chocolates for the crying boy, came home, and set him free.

When her holiday in the sun was over, Mary got back to work. The 1890s was her most productive decade. Just as they were years of discovery for Belle Époque France, they were years of discovery for Mary Cassatt. At her second solo show, in 1893, she exhibited a staggering total of ninety-eight works—sixty-seven prints, seventeen oils, and fourteen pastels.

Her art at this time showed an impressive diversity. It ranged from the delicate, small-scale prints to large-scale paintings inspired by the Chicago mural. But both prints and paintings continued the theme of women picking the symbolic "fruits of knowledge."

Cassatt also introduced a newer theme—women alone, lost in thought. For these pictures, Mary used a model whose broad shoulders, stocky neck, small eyes, and reddened ears did not conform to popular notions of beauty. When a friend criticized the "coarseness" of her model, Mary explained that she had never worshiped surface prettiness: "Everyone has their criterion of beauty. I confess I love health & strength."

In 1894 Cassatt branched out even further

when she painted the unusual picture *The Boating Party*. It is one of her few works to include a male figure, and it is one of her rare water scenes. In the painting, a darkly dressed man is rowing a woman and child in a boat. Bright patches of color—yellow boat, blue water—give a Japanese flavor to the scene. The composition of the picture is tightly organized, with curving lines and straight lines leading the viewer's eyes to the boat's passengers. The three people in the boat watch each other closely. *The Boating Party*, with its mysterious glances and tense energy, is widely regarded as one of Mary's masterpieces. Years later she would write to Durand-Ruel, "I do not want to sell it. I have already promised it to my family."

In France, Mary received heaps of praise for her achievements. In the press she was credited with "skill that reminds us of Manet, Renoir, and her master [teacher] and friend Degas." From time to time, there came a "left-handed compliment," too. One reviewer felt that Cassatt's great powers of observation proved that she possessed "all the qualities of an honest man." How annoyed Mary was when critics showed surprise at a woman's talent!

Praise—of any kind—generated sales. And profits from the sale of her work allowed Mary to buy her own home. Built in 1783 in the fertile

The Boating Party, *considered one of Cassatt's masterpieces*

valley of the Oise River, it was called Château de Beaufresne (Beautiful Ash Tree). The big old brick house lived up to its name, for it was surrounded by forty-five acres of green lawns, gardens, and majestic trees. Now Mary no longer had to search for a country place to rent each summer. And Château de Beaufresne was only forty miles from Paris, conveniently close to the Cassatts' apartment at 10, rue de Marignan.

The three-story house was run down when Mary bought it. She threw herself into the task of turning it into a home. "I ask myself when will I find the time to do a bit of painting!" she wrote to Durand-Ruel. Renovation took too long, and Mary

Château de Beaufresne, Mary's country home

almost put Beaufresne back on the market. But things gradually sorted themselves out, and the house was made comfortable and up-to-date.

Mary put in running water and new bathrooms. "I hope I am now nearly up to the American standard," she joked to a friend. "I need not say that I am so far beyond my French neighbors that they think I am demented." The rooms at Beaufresne were decorated to Mary's taste, with cozy places to sit and an assortment of antiques. Some of the old furniture she painted a cheerful shade of green. She lined the walls with Japanese wood-block prints, pictures by Courbet and by her friends—Degas, Pissarro, Morisot, and Cézanne.

The grounds of Beaufresne also reflected Mary's taste. She planted a vegetable garden with asparagus, strawberries, tomatoes, and the American corn that she had missed so much. She stocked the pond with trout, which guests could

catch and eat for dinner. And after much preparation, Mary began a rose garden that would eventually contain more than one thousand plants. She tended every phase of the roses' growth and loved their sweet smell and vivid colors. She used her artist's eye to group the flowers and discovered that "there is nothing like making pictures with real things."

But Mary's mother was ill again, too ill to enjoy the fruit trees and flowers of Beaufresne. In 1895 Mary wrote a sad letter: "I often nurse [Mother] for weeks at a time . . . life seems very dark to me just now." On October 21, seventy-nine-year-old Katherine Cassatt died.

For Mary this was a crushing blow, and her grief was almost unbearable. A light had gone out of her life forever. Her mother's intelligence, courage, and warmth had always been a shining example to Mary. Mother and daughter had understood each other well. And for eighteen years they had been companions in a foreign land. Now, for the first time since 1877, Mary was alone—the only member of the Cassatt family left in France.

Katherine Cassatt had often worried about her daughter's being left alone. She had once told Aleck, "After all a woman who is not married is lucky if she has a decided love for work of any kind and the more absorbing the better." Mrs. Cassatt would have been relieved to know that, in spite of her sorrow, Mary continued to be absorbed in her work. From 1895 on, Mary concentrated on the subject that had already become her trademark—mothers and children.

People have wondered why Mary Cassatt focused on this theme. Was it because pictures of mothers and children sold well in the late nineteenth century? Was it because Mary yearned for children and had none of her own? Or did the pictures reflect her deep love for her own mother? Perhaps all three reasons apply.

Sticking to one topic suited Cassatt's perfectionist work habits, too. She agreed with Degas when he said, "It is essential to do the same subject over again, ten times, a hundred times. In art nothing must appear accidental." Now using mostly pastels, Mary explored this universal relationship. She depicted mothers cuddling their children, comforting them, washing and feeding them, reading to them, and simply admiring them. Some of the pictures have a solid color for background, some have patterned wallpaper, and some show details of a chair, a mirror, or a jug. Cassatt's genius was such that she created a unique scene each time, even as she used the same theme.

The Bath, which shows a mother washing her little girl's feet, is one of the most powerful of the mother-and-child works. Its luscious colors and patterns make a strong impact. The stripes of the mother's dress—lavender, green, and white—contrast with the multicolored carpet. The green-painted furniture that Mary liked is in the background. Cassatt's composition tells a story of closeness between the woman and child. Their dark heads are touching, and the mother holds her daughter's small foot in her hand.

The Bath was not painted to show off female beauty, as were many works by male artists of the day. Instead, Cassatt painted individuals as they really looked, beautiful or not. Her strength was in her ability to describe relationships. And she brought her keen insight to the special bond between women and their children. She observed them in their private moments, in the midst of their daily lives, in their quiet love.

Art collectors eagerly invested in Mary's unsentimental pictures. Some of her old friends were also, finally, enjoying success. For by the 1890s, Impressionist painters had gained a measure of hard-won acceptance. Degas's brilliantly colored pastels were in demand. Renoir was no longer starving, and Monet was becoming positively rich.

Pissarro was one of the few original Independents who were still struggling. As late as 1894, he lamented to his son, "I am broke, completely broke." Cassatt was distressed by her friend's poverty. She tried to find students for him to teach, and she urged Durand-Ruel to promote his wonderful work. Pissarro took heart: "I hope Miss Cassatt will get something of mine sold, she liked my three canvases very much."

Mary was also distressed to see Degas's growing depression. His problem was not financial; he was terrified because he was slowly going blind. "Ah! Sight! Sight! Sight! . . . the difficulty of seeing makes me feel numb," he wrote. As his eyesight failed, the determined artist turned to sculptures of horses and ballerinas because he could feel them with his hands. But he was bitter, and he was embarrassed by the odd-looking glasses he had to wear. He began to turn away from his friends and isolate himself in his apartment, which was crammed, from top to bottom, with paintings. His housekeeper, Zoë, shooed more and more visitors away from his door.

Degas's friendship with Mary Cassatt suffered, too, because of an event that damaged many friendships in France—the Dreyfus Affair. In 1894 Alfred Dreyfus, a Jewish army officer, was accused of betraying French military secrets to the Germans. He was sentenced to life imprisonment on the dreaded Devil's Island. The evidence used to convict him was a certain letter, supposedly written by Dreyfus. But even when the letter was found to be in the handwriting of a Count Esterhazy, Dreyfus still was not set free. The French military officials—who had used the Jewish officer as a scapegoat—refused to admit their mistake.

The Dreyfus Affair created a furor in France, and it aroused Cassatt's strong sense of justice. According to Louisine Havemeyer, Mary felt that "France's honor was at stake." She joined Monet, the writer Émile Zola, and about 3,000 others in signing a pro-Dreyfus petition. The unfortunate man was given a second trial in 1899 but was not officially declared innocent until 1906.

Degas had sided with the aristocratic leaders of the army. His position led Pissarro, who was Jewish, to call Degas "the ferocious anti-Semite." The quarrel between Mary and Degas over the Dreyfus episode was deep, and the two did not speak to each other for a long time.

For Mary Cassatt, the 1890s had been a roller coaster of highs and lows. Her first one-woman exhibits had brought her to the peak of her fame. The works that she displayed—the color prints and the paintings dealing with women's lives—were products of Mary's middle age. Yet many were as daring as the creations of a twenty-year-old. The artist's will to experiment had taken her far. And the recognition Mary received made her intensely happy. ("Women should be *someone* and not *something*.")

But the deaths of her parents had plunged Mary into the deepest sorrow. The loss of her mother, especially, put Mary into a state of "great trouble," and she had to fight her way up from black depression.

When Mrs. Cassatt died, Gardner's family came to France and stayed for two years. Along with Mary, they divided their time between the Paris apartment and Château de Beaufresne. Young Gardner now had a baby sister, Ellen Mary. The newest Cassatt had been named after her Aunt Mary, and she quickly became the artist's favorite niece. *Ellen Mary Cassatt in a White Coat* is one of the striking portraits that resulted from the visit.

When the Philadelphia Cassatts sailed back home, Mary was alone again. The halls of Beaufresne and the rooms in Paris echoed with silence. With every ounce of her being, Mary missed Lydia, her father, and her mother. But as she had all her life, she took comfort in her work. One day Mary would explain her feelings to Louisine Havemeyer this way: "How we try for happiness, poor things, and how we don't find it; the best cure is hard work."

Chapter Nine

"I Am American"

"I am American. Simply and frankly American," Mary told her biographer Achille Ségard. She had not forgotten her roots. And though she had lived all her adult life in France, Cassatt claimed Philadelphia as her legal residence. In 1898, with no family cares to hold her back, she took a trip home—her first visit there since 1870, after the outbreak of the Franco-Prussian War. Mary's first stop was Philadelphia. But were her hometown journalists aware of her stature as an artist?

Some were. An article in the *Daily Evening Telegraph* announced, "She is one of the brilliant galaxy of cosmopolitan painters whose fame is worldwide and who are citizens of the world of art." And some definitely were not. A writer for the *Philadelphia Ledger* missed the point: "Mary Cassatt, sister of Mr. Cassatt, president of the Pennsylvania

Railroad, returned from Europe yesterday. She has been studying painting in France and owns the smallest Pekingese dog in the world." Mary had exhibited several times in her native city, but few Philadelphians were buying her pictures. Most of the Cassatt works in town had been gifts from the artist herself and hung on the walls of her relatives' homes.

She could not stay with Aleck. Her relationship with his wife, Lois, had grown steadily colder after the deaths of Mr. and Mrs. Cassatt. Sadly, the freeze between the two women made it harder for Mary to see her now-adult nieces and nephews—Eddie, Katharine, Robbie, and Elsie. So while in Philadelphia, Mary lived with Gard's family. Amid a flurry of relatives, she completed pastel portraits of young Gardner, Ellen Mary, and the newest baby, Eugenia.

Cassatt seldom painted portraits of people outside her family because she disliked the pressure of having to please them. (She remembered the to-do over Mrs. Riddle's nose.) But in America she made an exception to her rule. She traveled with her little Belgian griffon (not Pekingese!) to Boston to paint the children of Mr. and Mrs. Gardiner Hammond. Later Mary went to Connecticut, where she completed pastels of members of the Whittemore family.

At formal dinner parties in Boston, Cassatt pushed the cause of "our little band of Independents." Every glittering social event became an opportunity to create buyers of French Impressionist work. A quick look around the city had convinced Mary that Bostonians were indifferent to art. Of the Boston Museum she wrote, "The state the pictures are in is a disgrace to the Directors." In her view, a well-stocked museum was not a luxury; it was a necessity. It was especially important for young people to see beautiful pictures. Art could teach them to "admire good work and give the desire to be perfect in some one thing." Mary longed for the day when students would not have to go to Europe, as she had done, to see great paintings.

Before returning to France, Cassatt visited Henry and Louisine Havemeyer in their sumptuous new mansion in New York City. The "Sugar King's" house was filled with every kind of luxury: furniture decorated with gold leaf, Tiffany glass, priceless rugs. There was a music room hung with Chinese embroideries—and a magnificent gallery for art. As Mary walked through the gallery, she could see in heavy gold frames many of the pictures she had found for the Havemeyers. It was a welcome change from the "artistic wasteland" of Boston.

To her delight, the Havemeyers invited Mary

to accompany them on a picture-buying tour of Europe. Louisine had relied on Cassatt's judgment ever since she paid $100 for her first Degas. Now, as the Havemeyers planned to spend more of their vast fortune on art, they needed Mary's advice again. Cassatt was about to become, in Louisine's words, the "fairy godmother" of one of the world's most splendid collections of art.

The little group, which also included Mrs. Havemeyer's sister, started its trip in Genoa, Italy. The friends toured the country by train, seeing a different city almost every day. It was the right time for a treasure hunt. In Europe in the early 1900s, many paintings by Old Masters were for sale, and many of these works were undervalued.

Mary Cassatt was like a detective. She led the Havemeyers from old shops to shabby palaces, where poor noblemen were selling their family heirlooms. She was a shrewd bargainer who could almost always spot a fake.

In her memoirs Louisine described the adventure: "Miss Cassatt had the 'flair' of an old hunter... Mr. Havemeyer had the true energy of a collector, while I—well, I had the time of my life." The group took time out to buy an antique ring for Mary, to ride the gondolas of Venice, and to picnic on bologna sandwiches near the town of Ravenna.

In Spain, Mary discovered irresistible paintings

by two artists who were then almost unknown in America—El Greco (1541–1614) and Goya (1746–1828). The bargaining for their work was fierce, and it was several years before El Greco's *View of Toledo* and *Assumption of the Virgin* and Goya's *The Majas on the Balcony* were shipped to America. (Today these pictures are considered to be among the finest masterpieces in the United States.)

And in Paris, Cassatt helped the Havemeyers build America's best collection of nineteenth-century French art. Louisine was captivated by Manet's pictures, "brilliant with life, gay with color." She and her husband would eventually own more than two dozen each of the works of Manet, Courbet, Monet, Cézanne, and, of course, Cassatt.

But it was the art of Degas that Mrs. Havemeyer loved the most. Mary often brought her to his studio, where she was one of the few people allowed to look through dusty stacks of the artist's drawings. While Louisine browsed, Degas and Cassatt gossiped and shared private jokes. Although Degas hated to part with his work, he sometimes selected pictures that he felt Louisine should have. The Havemeyers' collection would one day contain over sixty of Degas's oils, pastels, and drawings, and more than seventy of his sculptures.

"I am American," Mary said. And to one American collector she wrote, "It has been one of the chief interests of my life to help fine things across the Atlantic." She had taken time from her own work to advise the Havemeyers. After they returned to New York, Mary organized the restoring, framing, insuring, and shipping of their purchases. But it had all been worth it. For Mary knew that much of the collection would one day be donated to museums as a gift to the American people. (In 1929, Louisine Havemeyer did give most of the family's paintings to New York's Metropolitan Museum of Art, where they can be seen today.) And Louisine appreciated Mary's contribution: "She was the most devoted friend, the wisest counselor, the most faithful ally anyone ever had. Without her aid, I should never have been able to make the collection."

After looking at masterpieces in Italy, Spain, and France, Cassatt was itching to get back to her own studio. As she approached her sixties, she still held fast to her belief in hard work. It was the only thing that could fight loneliness: "I work, & that is the whole secret of anything like content with life, when everything else is gone." In the first decade of the new century, Mary was very busy.

She now had less interest in precise line and firmly modeled form. Instead, the oils, and pastels of this period are characterized by bold, free strokes of color. Paints and pastels were laid on thickly to make a textured surface. *Young Mother Sewing*, completed shortly after the European trip, clearly shows Cassatt's return to a more Impressionist type of brushwork.

In her mother-and-child pictures, Mary enjoyed including more than her usual amount of background detail—trees on sloping lawns, gardens spotted with flowers, glimpses of water and sky. She also indulged her lifelong passion for elegant clothes, dressing her models in fabrics of rich pattern and color.

An art critic writing in a French magazine called Mary Cassatt "one of the foremost pastellists of the time." She had loved the medium since her early Impressionist days and, like Degas, was wonderfully skilled at handling the chalky sticks of color. In the 1900s, Mary began a pastel series of children alone—little girls in fancy, oversized hats. *Simone in a White Bonnet, Child with Red Hat, Child in Orange Dress*, and many others are composed of splashes of bright color, sparked with white. The pictures avoid too much "sweetness" because each one is also a perceptive study of the mood of the girl in the hat.

These appealing pastels were among Mary's best-selling works. They practically "flew" out of her studio. With the help of Durand-Ruel and a new dealer, Ambroise Vollard, Cassatt's public was rapidly growing. (Vollard even persuaded her to sell a number of pastels that were not yet finished.) There were solo exhibits in Paris and London. And to Mary's satisfaction, her work was also being shown throughout the United States—from New York to Minneapolis to Portland, Oregon. Her 1898 trip, as well as the efforts of her dealers, had finally established Cassatt's reputation across the sea.

Now that American art officials were aware of Mary Cassatt's work, they began to offer her honors and prizes. In 1904 her oil *The Caress* was judged the best figure painting at the annual show at Mary's old school the Pennsylvania Academy of the Fine Arts. It was awarded the Lippincott Prize. One year later *The Caress* received the Harris Prize from the Art Institute of Chicago. But Cassatt was angry that Durand-Ruel had lent her picture to these juried, competitive exhibits. And she was upset that the Americans were copying the old Salon system of the French.

Mary firmly refused the awards. In letters to both institutions, she took care to explain why she stuck to her principles: "I was one of the original 'Independents' who founded a society where there was to be no jury, no medals, no awards. . . . Of course unless you had lived in Paris and seen the ill effects of official exhibitions you can hardly understand how strongly we felt."

But the directors of the Pennsylvania Academy seemed not to understand. After Mary rejected their award, they asked her to serve on an art jury! She patiently wrote that she could never bear to turn down the work of a fellow painter, no matter how "humble." No one, she believed, had the right to do so: "Why should my judgement be taken? Or any one elses for that matter." Cassatt charged that the jury system discouraged new ideas, whereas "in art what we want is the certainty that the one spark of original genius shall not be extinguished." Mary listed the names of colleagues whose talent had been ignored by juries for years.

Although she would not accept honors that did not conform to her principles, she appreciated the attention from her native land. Because of it, she embarked on her second public art project for an American city. Mary painted two mother-and-child *tondos* (circular pictures) for a grand new state capitol building in Harrisburg, Pennsylvania. But again, Cassatt's principles ruled her actions. She heard that tax money meant for the building was being stolen by politicians and others. Although she considered the *tondos* among her best pictures, she immediately withdrew them from the project.

In 1904 the French government invited Mary Cassatt to join its most prestigious society, the Legion of Honor. Its members were selected for individual merit—and very few were women. Because this award did not pit one person against another, Mary accepted it and wore the Legion's red ribbon proudly. Also in line with Mary's principles was the post of honorary president of the Art League in Paris. At the Art League she gave lectures and set up a scholarship for each year's two most promising students.

When Cassatt grew tired of life in Paris, she retreated to peaceful Beaufresne. In the country she could relax and enjoy the changing seasons. She loved the lush rain of springtime and the green days of summer. And she reflected on the fall, "in these warm still September days it is lovely."

In her painting room on the ground floor, she worked all day, dressed in a white smock. Sometimes she painted outside by the trout pond, where weeping willows bent down to the water. The result of one such afternoon is the enchanting picture *Summertime*, in which two women in a rowboat are admiring a cluster of white ducks. In Mary's view, "The whole beauty of the place is in the water."

Her parents and sister were gone, but Beaufresne was far from empty. The big house was run by the faithful Mathilde, who kept Mary company, took care of her clothes, and did her hair. Mathilde was the lucky recipient of dozens of paintings that her employer was not quite satisfied with. "Here, Taudy, you can have this; it's no good," Mary would say. There was also a housemaid, a cook, three gardeners, and Pierre, who drove the horse and carriage. In 1906 Pierre's title changed from "coachman" to "chauffeur" because the Havemeyers gave Mary her first car, a Renault.

Every day after work, Cassatt put on her plumed hat and veil and went for a bumpy ride in the Renault. She always took the same route, stopping at the nearby village of Mesnil-Théribus to find models for her pictures. Mary liked to paint the same subject many times in order to perfect her technique, and was glad that some of her models learned to relax and pose quite naturally after several sittings. One such willing model was a little girl named Margot Lux. She appears in the pastel *Margot in Blue* and in about two dozen other pictures by Cassatt. Mary found the women of Mesnil-Théribus to be ideal models for her mother-and-child pictures. Unlike richer women, they had not left their children in the care of nursemaids. They held their babies with the same ease that Mary wanted to convey in her pictures.

The more time Cassatt spent at Beaufresne,

the more involved she became in local affairs. She gave money to the village school. And when she realized that the button factory at Mesnil was underpaying the local women, she took action. She hired some of the women to work at Beaufresne and found jobs for others in the homes of her friends.

In both Paris and the country, Mary enjoyed visitors of all kinds. In her sixties, she was still happy to juggle the demands of social life and work. She greeted her friends warmly, with a pack of noisy Belgian griffons at her heels. Dinners were delicious, and for dessert Mathilde made chocolate caramels. At Beaufresne guests enjoyed the treats while sitting in a sunny, glassed-in gallery overlooking the lawn.

Tall, very thin, straight as a soldier—in her high-necked dress and amethyst jewelry—Mary Cassatt was the center of every gathering. Her conversation was spicy and brilliant, and she gestured with her hands as she spoke. With Georges Clemenceau (twice premier of France), Cassatt argued about politics. She loved the novels of Tolstoy and Mark Twain, whom she discussed with her writer friends. The Durand-Ruels, Ambroise Vollard, the Havemeyers, and Mary's many relatives were frequent guests. Artists—several of them from Philadelphia—came to Cassatt for advice.

The years had not softened Mary's sharp opinions. One American art student, Alan Philbrick, called her "a fiery and peppery lady." He added, "I was scared to death of her." Another young man remembered that Cassatt would bang her fist on the table to make a point. She urged all the students to learn by copying the Old Masters, as she had done. She also expressed her disgust with the latest developments in early twentieth-century art. To Mary, the innovations of Matisse and Picasso were nothing but a gimmick. "No Frenchman of any standing in the art world has ever taken any of these things seriously," she declared.

Mary Cassatt believed that art had not progressed much after reaching a high point with the genius of her friend Degas. She missed the exciting days when she had been part of the revolution in art. It upset her that just as prices for Impressionist paintings were soaring, many of the "little band of Independents" were already dead. Those who remained were struggling with the problems of old age. Renoir was crippled with arthritis and had difficulty holding his brush. Monet had a cataract (a clouding of the lens) in one eye. By 1909, Degas would, tragically, be forced to give up painting, having gone nearly blind.

And once again, a series of deaths shook Mary's world. Her beloved niece Katharine, daugh-

Mary at Château de Beaufresne, holding one of her Belgian griffons

ter of Aleck and Lois, died at the age of thirty-four. One year later, in 1906, Aleck himself died. Mary's oldest brother had been a great source of strength to her all her life, and she was devastated: "I feel as if a force had gone out of my life and left me so much weaker." Mary received another shock the following year when Henry O. Havemeyer suddenly died. She had cared very much for Henry, her fellow traveler, and she cabled the grieving Louisine, "I too mourn a friend." Such was Mary's devotion to family and friends that she crossed the ocean in 1908 to spend Christmas with the bereaved. (Mary's seasickness on this trip was so severe that she never again risked a visit to America.)

As family members died, Mary's friends became increasingly dear to her. One new friend was Theodate Pope of Connecticut. Theodate was a professional architect and, as a woman of unusual achievement, had much in common with Mary Cassatt. Like Mary, she had avoided the social whirl of the well-to-do and had chosen a life of serious work.

The two friends exchanged lively letters containing witty arguments about art and politics. They shared an interest in women's rights and supported the cause of women's suffrage (the right to vote). And they believed that the key to a young girl's future lay in a top-notch education. When

Theodate started a girls' boarding school in Connecticut, Cassatt's niece Eugenia enrolled. "Isn't it splendid to be able to influence whole generations?" exclaimed Mary.

Because both women had lost loved ones (Theodate's fiancé had died at the age of twenty-six), they were fascinated by spiritualism—the investigation into life after death. Spiritualism was popular at the time. It was also of interest to many well-respected psychologists. Mary and Theodate read widely on the subject. When Theodate came to Paris, the two friends attended a séance in an effort to "see through the mysterious veil" that separates the living from the dead. Remarkably, the practical-minded Cassatt was completely won over. After another séance, she reported seeing a table rise four feet off the floor—by itself. Her belief in the possibility of communicating with the dead was rooted in her firm faith that "life is going on though we cannot see it."

Mary was linked to the Pope family by art, as well as by friendship. Theodate's parents, with a fortune made in the steel industry, had begun buying Impressionist paintings back in the 1890s. In the 1900s, Mary gladly advised them on new purchases. Hill-Stead, the Popes' home in Farmington, Connecticut, designed by Theodate herself, is now a gem of a small museum.

Another valued friend of Mary's was James Stillman, chairman of the board of New York's National City Bank. In 1909 he retired, left his homes in New York and Rhode Island, and settled permanently in France. His enormous house in Paris, surrounded by gardens, was as luxurious as the Havemeyers' mansion in New York. To Mary, its walls cried out for pictures!

James Stillman was not as passionate about paintings as the Havemeyers were. However, just as he had set himself the task of learning French, he was willing to learn about art. Mary steered him toward the Old Masters and the French Impressionists. When she saw a picture that she thought he should have, she summoned him right away. Stillman was cautious about buying, though, and always made sure that he didn't spend a penny too much. But Cassatt assured him that "there is no better investment than a 'work of art.'" The Stillman mansion soon contained Impressionist paintings (many by Cassatt) and works by Gainsborough, Ingres, Titian, and Rembrandt. Many of these were later given by Stillman's heirs to the Metropolitan Museum of Art.

Like Mary Cassatt, James Stillman lived alone. (He was separated from his wife.) Many people were afraid of Stillman, the stern, hard-driving perfectionist. But not Mary. "Miss Cassatt was the only person who dared tease Father," said Stillman's son, Ernest. The banker was attracted to Mary's elegance. He also respected her intelligence and her fearlessness. Stillman became Cassatt's biggest fan and probably asked her to marry him. But their relationship was sometimes stormy. After one fight, Stillman sent Mary a present from Tiffany's—a jeweled bowl and collar for her dog!

In spite of the occasional storms, Cassatt and Stillman enjoyed each other's company. They had spirited discussions on women's suffrage. They had long, delicious lunches at Beaufresne. And the two friends loved to sightsee. They spent happy days touring the French countryside in Stillman's comfortable car. In winter they went to Mary's rented house, Villa Angeletto, in the south of France. Besides Degas, James Stillman was the only male outside her family that Mary had ever asked to paint.

In the fall of 1910, Mary packed her suitcases for a two-month trip to Egypt with Gard and Jennie, sixteen-year-old Ellen Mary, and thirteen-year-old Eugenia. First the group met in Paris and traveled to Munich, Germany, and Vienna, Austria. Then they took the luxurious train the Orient Express through Hungary and Bulgaria and down to Constantinople (modern-day Istanbul, Turkey). In Constantinople, Mary wrote Theodate

Mary Cassatt (far right) and Gardner Cassatt with his wife and two daughters, photographed by James Stillman at Versailles in 1910

Pope a cheerful letter: "It seems so odd not to be working all day, but seeing sights & enjoying the young friends of my nieces." She welcomed the break from her routine and loved the lighthearted company of Ellen Mary and Eugenia.

From Turkey the travelers proceeded to Cairo, Egypt. There, in high spirits, the Cassatts boarded the Egyptian boat *Hope* and began their voyage up the Nile. They saw the ancient pyramids, the Temple of Luxor, and, by moonlight, the awesome Temple of Karnak. But all too soon, being cooped up on a boat got on everyone's nerves. Mary compared boat life to prison life. She began to feel bored by the endless tombs and temples. She could not even set up her paints because a harsh desert wind whipped across the river. "I am pining to get back to work," she wrote to Louisine. "There are things I am dying to do."

Mary's feeling moved swiftly from boredom to fear because Gard had taken to his bed with a fever. And though seven doctors in turn visited the boat, he was getting sicker. Mary was frantic with worry. All she could do was watch the hired nurse. "I feel so utterly helpless, and I am."

The Cassatts hurried back to Paris as fast as they could, but by the time they arrived, Gard had developed pleurisy (an inflammation of the lining of the lungs). On April 5, 1911, Mary Cassatt's last sibling died. She never fully recovered from this death: "Now I am the only one left in my family! Who would have believed that both my brothers would go so near to each other."

She made a brave effort to pick up the pieces of her life: "There is no use looking back," she wrote. "I must try to get strong again and get to work." She spent the winter in the warm sun at Villa Angeletto, with James Stillman trying to comfort her. But at sixty-seven, Mary could not bounce back quickly from disaster. In addition to depression, she now suffered from diabetes. On a strict diet to control the disease, Mary saw her weight plunge temporarily to eighty-six pounds. Haunted by sleepless nights, loneliness, and pain, Cassatt could not work for almost two years.

No sooner had her health improved than she received another blow. Mary found that, like Degas, she would have to face the worst enemy of all—blindness. She had begun to develop cataracts in both eyes.

Mary's sight was weakening gradually, and she was tired. "I have worked so hard . . . and nothing takes it out of one like painting," she confided to Louisine in 1913. But she was not ready to give up. She threw herself back into her art, knowing that she was running out of time. James Stillman worried about his friend: "She has had a long illness and is not as young as she was—but no one, not even Mathilde, can stop her."

These were Cassatt's last years of work. She could not see well enough for the exacting discipline of printmaking. And though she did not realize it, her failing eyesight had caused a striking decline in the quality of her oils and pastels. Her colors had become harsh; her lines had grown sloppy.

James Stillman had been right. Neither he nor Mathilde nor anyone else could stop Mary Cassatt. But loss of vision finally did. An eye operation was only slightly successful, and by 1915, she could no longer see clearly enough to work. Even as she put away her paints and pastels, she hoped to find a doctor who could cure her. But Mary Cassatt was never to work again.

Chapter Ten

War and Roses

The summer of 1914 began quietly for Mary, with relatives visiting Beaufresne. Robbie Cassatt was there with his two sons, as well as Ellen Mary, Eugenia, and their mother. The girls took French lessons, and everyone enjoyed long walks around the grounds of the château. The family had heard much talk of war, but no one suspected that the peace of France's Belle Époque was in its last days.

Then on June 28, Archduke Francis Ferdinand, heir to the throne of Austria-Hungary, was assassinated at Sarajevo. His murder triggered a chain reaction in which, one by one, the nations of Europe were dragged into the "Great War" (World War I). The old established order of Europe broke up. Most people thought that the war would be over in a few months. But the Allies (France, Britain, Russia, and by 1917, the United States) were to fight the Central Powers (Germany,

Mary Cassatt in her plumed hat in 1914, the year World War I began

Austria-Hungary, and Turkey) for four bloody years.

By August 1914, the German army had swept into Belgium and France. Château de Beaufresne was soon in the military zone, with fighting occurring only fifty miles away. From her house, Mary could hear the boom of the big guns, and the French authorities ordered all civilians to leave the area. (Because Mathilde Vallet was German, she had to leave the country altogether.) The Havemeyers begged Mary to come to the safety of New York. But her sense of duty—and her dread of seasickness—would not permit Mary to leave France. She chose instead to wait out the war years in the south of France, at Villa Angeletto.

As the war ripped up Europe, Mary wrote to a friend in the United States, "The world is mad just now, when is it to end—" It was the most horrible war anyone had yet seen. Soldiers lived and fought in muddy, stinking trenches and faced a frightening array of new weapons. In fact, World War I was a war of "firsts": the first submachine guns, the first armored tanks, the first bomber planes, and the first use of poison gas. When the slaughter finally ended, in 1918, 10 million young men were dead.

Cassatt was touched directly by the war when a German submarine torpedoed the British passenger ship the *Lusitania*, in 1915. Theodate Pope had been one of the 128 Americans on board. She managed to survive, although more than 1,000 men, women, and children drowned. "My dear dear Theodate," wrote a shaken Mary, "If you were saved it is because you have still something to do in this World— As long as we live we do not know to what usages we are to be put." The attack on the ship enraged many Americans. "Remember the *Lusitania*!" became a popular cry, and the incident influenced the United States' decision to enter the war.

Mary was deeply moved by all the suffering. She saw the wounded limping home; she heard stories about soldiers with their eyes shot out. So, as sad as she was about her own fading eyesight, she did not give in to self-pity: "In this sea of misery in which we live, an individual case seems of little account. There are ten thousand blind in France." Cassatt did all she could to help, generously giving money to war widows and to soldiers' hospitals.

During the war, she was intensely lonely. Normal entertaining was impossible, and Mary was completely cut off from relatives and friends in America. (German submarines had made the ocean too dangerous to cross.) "I never felt so isolated in my life as I do now," she wrote to Louisine. "Your letters are the only things that have made me feel not altogether abandoned." From time to time, Mary received permission to return to Beaufresne and her Paris apartment. At each visit, she was glad to see that her property had not been destroyed. The artist was constantly worried about the safety of the paintings inside both her homes. She was worried about James Stillman's collection in Paris, too. But as always, she put her own concerns into perspective. More than anything, Mary was worried about the future of the world, the world that her nieces and nephews and their children would inherit.

She was as sure of her opinions on world affairs as she was of her views on art. She felt that men had made a shocking mess of things and that another such war would mean the end of civilization. Mary thought that it was up to women, with their less warlike natures, to band together and work for peace. With millions of fathers, husbands, and sons away at war or dead on the battlefields, women had already become more active outside their homes. Now it was more important than ever that they insist on their right to vote. (French women, as well as American, did not yet have this right.) Men might even be relieved if women assumed part of the political burden, thought Mary.

On the other side of the Atlantic, Louisine Havemeyer had joined the National Woman's Party and was giving impassioned speeches in favor of women's suffrage. She was also planning a large art exhibit, with admission fees to be donated to the cause. Cassatt wholeheartedly supported the plan and lent several of her paintings, old and new. She asked a collector to lend to the exhibit one of his works by Degas, telling him, "The sight of that picture may be a turning point in the life of some young American painter. The first sight of Degas pictures was the turning point of my artistic life."

The Suffrage Loan Exhibition opened in New York in 1915. Its focus was unusual—the Havemeyers' Old Masters alongside works by Degas and Cassatt. Even at seventy-one, Mary was awed at having her art displayed next to that of her brilliant old friend. But she took comfort in knowing that, although she had learned much from Degas, she had never copied him. Her work was her own. *Lady at the Tea Table*, so long hidden away, was at the exhibit. Two French museums offered to buy the portrait, but Cassatt turned them down. She demonstrated her commitment to American collections by selling *Lady* to the Metropolitan Museum of Art instead.

In spite of the high quality of the paintings, the exhibition was a flop. Mary was disgusted at the poor attendance. Many well-to-do, well-educated New Yorkers had stayed away from the show because of its radical political purpose—women's suffrage. However, complete victory for the suffragists was only five years away. The Nineteenth

Amendment to the U.S. Constitution, which gave women the right to vote, would be passed by Congress in 1919 and ratified by the states one year later. (The same right would not be granted to French women until the 1940s.)

In these years, Mary saw very little of Degas. By the early 1900s, he had cut himself off from almost everyone. As his few remaining friends died, he looked back on his life with melancholy. Degas, who had lived only for his art, told Ambroise Vollard, "A man should marry. You don't know what the solitude of old age is like."

When he could no longer work, this great artist wandered blind and alone through the streets of Paris. He even took to following funeral processions as they wound their way to the graveyard. He seemed to long for death.

Kind and loyal Mary Cassatt was horrified at Degas's decline. She convinced his niece, Jeanne Fèvre, to stay with her uncle and care for him. And in his last illness, it was Mary who arranged for a bedside nurse. Degas died in 1917 at the age of eighty-three. His country—caught up in war—hardly noticed his death. Mary wrote to Louisine, "Of course you have seen that Degas is no more. We buried him on Saturday, a beautiful sunshine, a little crowd of friends and admirers, all very quiet and peaceful in the midst of this dreadful upheaval of which he was barely conscious."

There followed several sales of the jumbled contents of Degas's studio—his own work and other artists' work that he had collected. Cassatt arranged for Louisine Havemeyer to buy the graceful little statue *The Dancer*. She was pleased to see Degas's art fetching extremely high prices. She was also pleased when the dealers found a picture she had done, *Girl Arranging Her Hair*, and thought it had been painted by Degas!

After the war, Mary took up her old life in Paris and at Beaufresne. Mathilde rejoined her, and Mary hired a new chauffeur, Armand Delaporte. In 1921 another cataract operation proved unsuccessful. Now Cassatt could no longer see to read and could barely see to write, although she struggled on with her letters. Her frustration at not being able to paint was immense: "It is the impossibility of doing anything that is so wearing on the nerves, to me especially who lived only for my work."

It was Mary's frustration that caused her to break off her relationship with Louisine Havemeyer. One day in 1923, Mathilde cleaned out the closet in Mary's painting room and found twenty-five copperplates that had been etched in the drypoint method. Cassatt was not able to see them, but her printer, M. Delatre, assured her that the plates had never before been printed. Excited at this unexpected find, Mary had them printed and sent to Louisine in New York. But when William Ivins, curator at the Metropolitan Museum, saw the drypoints, he realized that the plates had actually been used years ago. They could not honestly be sold as "new."

"I have no respect for the opinion of Mr. Ivins," shouted Mary, positive that she was right. She was equally furious with Louisine for agreeing with the curator. Although Louisine remained understanding, Mary never again spoke or wrote to her oldest friend. Another link with the past had been broken.

Cassatt spent her last years quietly at Château de Beaufresne. She was still keenly interested in the lives of her young relatives in America and sent them letters in her shaky handwriting. Almost every day Armand Delaporte took Mary for a ride in the Renault. Mary also took pleasure in her beautiful roses. Even though she could hardly see them, she insisted on cutting them herself and setting out bouquets for guests.

The visitors who came in the 1920s found Mary much changed. She was nearly blind, sick with diabetes, and terribly lonely. And like Degas in the frailty of old age, she had some regrets. She told a friend that she had given up having children in order to paint: "A woman artist must be . . . capable of making the primary sacrifices."

Yet flashes of her younger self shone through. Over tea and cake, she argued excitedly about politics and art. And she was concerned about the future of her relatives and her home. It comforted Mary to write a will that left Beaufresne to her niece Ellen Mary, because the young woman loved the peaceful place as much as she herself did.

A month after her eighty-second birthday, on June 14, 1926, Mary Cassatt died. Her beloved nieces and nephews were far away in America on that warm summer night. Mary died leaning on the arm of her chauffeur. Mathilde was at her side. Because she had been a member of the French Legion of Honor, she was given a funeral with military honors. A large crowd of friends and neighbors came, and the local band played in the rain. As the procession reached the cemetery, the sun came out, and after prayers were said, the mourners scattered roses over Mary's grave.

❖ ❖ ❖

Edgar Degas had once said, "One continues to the last day figuring things out. It is very fortunate that it should be so." So it was with Mary Cassatt. She belonged to that small, special group of people who devote their days to creating beautiful pictures. And from her teen years to her old age, her life was a journey with that one purpose. The journey was joyous, but it was also lonely and hard.

Mary needed all her courage to see it through.

Like many of her paintings, Cassatt herself was a study in contrasts. She was a "prim and proper" nineteenth-century lady; she was an intense woman who fled to France for her career—a career in the newest art of her day. She was modest, yet she had unshakable faith in herself. She was fiercely outspoken, but she was also kind.

Mary was passionate about art, and she was passionate about people. She applied her wonderful skill to recording the mysteries of the human face. In a harmony of line and color, she also told the age-old story of the bond between mother and child. Her exquisite oils, pastels, and prints are a delight to the eye, and they have earned her a place among the great artists of the world.

She would be happy if she could see that generations of people have loved her pictures, which hang in museums throughout the world. She would be especially happy that much of her work can be found in *American* museums, where it forms part of the fine Impressionist collections that she worked so hard to build.

Mary Cassatt was a perfectionist, though, and was never completely satisfied. Perhaps she would repeat something that she wrote at the age of seventy-six: "I have not done what I wanted to but I tried to make a good fight of it."

Appendix One
Mary Cassatt: A Time Line

1844—Mary Cassatt is born on May 22 in the town of Allegheny City, Pennsylvania.

1848—The Cassatt family moves to a house called Hardwick in the countryside near Lancaster, Pennsylvania. Here Mary learns to ride a horse.

1849—The family moves to Philadelphia, but keeps Hardwick as a country home.

1851—The Cassatts sail to Europe to further Alexander's (Aleck's) education and to find medical care for Robert (Robbie).

1855—Robbie dies of his bone disease in Prussia. Mary visits the Paris Exposition Universelle, where she is exposed to French painting. The family then returns to Pennsylvania.

1860—Sixteen-year-old Mary enrolls at the Pennsylvania Academy of the Fine Arts, where she will spend four years.

1865—The Civil War ends, and Mary travels to Paris to study works of the Old Masters and to take painting lessons from Jean-Léon Gérôme and Charles Chaplin.

1868—Mary paints in the French countryside with her friend Eliza Haldeman. *La Mandoline (The Mandolin Player)* is Mary's first work to be accepted and shown at the Paris Salon.

1870—Mary returns to Pennsylvania because of the outbreak of the Franco-Prussian War.

1872—With the Franco-Prussian War over, Mary and her friend Emily Sartain go to paint in Parma, Italy. After Parma, Mary continues to study and paint in Italy and Spain.

1874—Mary settles permanently in Paris, where she meets Louisine Elder (Havemeyer). At the Paris Salon, Edgar Degas admires Cassatt's portrait *Madame Cortier*.

1875—Mary sees Edgar Degas's work for the first time.

1877—Degas asks Mary to join the Impressionist movement, and she accepts "with joy." The two artists begin a lifelong friendship. Mary's parents and sister, Lydia, come to live with her in Paris.

1879—Mary exhibits for the first time with the Impressionists, at the Fourth Impressionist Exhibit. She displays eleven works.

1880—Mary participates in the Fifth Impressionist Exhibit. She spends the summer with her nieces and nephews at Marly-le-Roi.

1881—Mary exhibits at the Sixth Impressionist Exhibit, and her pictures painted at Marly-le-Roi are a huge success.

1882—Lydia dies on November 7 of kidney disease. Because of disputes within the Impressionist movement, Cassatt and Degas boycott the Seventh Impressionist Exhibit.

1886—Mary helps fund and takes part in the Eighth—and last—Impressionist Exhibit in France. Her work is also represented at New York's first major Impressionist exhibit, organized by Paul Durand-Ruel.

1891—Cassatt's first one-woman show is held at the Paris gallery of Durand-Ruel. Her series of ten Japanese-style prints wins praise, notably from Degas and Pissarro. Mary's father, Robert Cassatt, dies on December 9.

1893—Mary's mural *Modern Woman* is displayed at Chicago's World's Columbian Exposition. She shows a total of ninety-eight works at her second one-woman show, in Paris.

1894—Cassatt moves with her mother to Château de Beaufresne, a beautiful country estate that Mary purchased with money from the sale of her work.

1895—Mary's mother, Katherine Cassatt, dies on October 21.

1898—Mary visits the United States for the first time since the Franco-Prussian War, in 1870. In Philadelphia, Boston, and New York, she tries to stimulate interest in French Impressionist art.

1901—Cassatt accompanies Henry and Louisine Havemeyer on a picture-buying tour of Italy, Spain, and France.

1904—The French government names Cassatt a member of the Legion of Honor, France's highest civilian award.

1906—Alexander (Aleck) Cassatt dies on December 28.

1908—Mary takes what is to be her last trip to the United States.

1910—Mary tours Egypt with her brother Gardner and his family.

1911—Having fallen sick in Egypt, Gardner dies in Paris on April 5.

1914—World War I begins, and Mary is cut off from American family and friends.

1915—Cassatt can no longer see well enough to work because of cataracts in both eyes; several operations are to do little good. Mary helps organize New York's Suffrage Loan Exhibition, the proceeds of which are to be used to help U.S. women gain the vote.

1917—Edgar Degas dies on September 27.

1923—Mary breaks off her friendship with Louisine Havemeyer because of a controversy over a set of Casatt's drypoint prints.

1926—Mary dies on June 14 and is buried near her beloved Château de Beaufresne, which she has bequeathed to her favorite niece, Ellen Mary Cassatt.

Appendix Two
Sources

Introduction
6: "I am not willing to admit:" Roudebush, *Cassatt*, p. 22.
7: "I would almost rather:" Mathews, *Mary Cassatt*, p. 13.

Chapter One: Paris and Pennsylvania
10: "dreadfully headstrong": Sweet, *Miss Mary Cassatt*, p. 81.
11: "The only being she": Hale, *Mary Cassatt*, p. 13.
12: "Mary was always a": Sweet, *Miss Mary Cassatt*, p. 20.
12: "We used to have": Sweet, *Miss Mary Cassatt*, p. 20.
14: "Our father did not have": Carson, *Mary Cassatt*, p. 4.

Chapter Two: "A Passion for Line and Color"
16: "Well, Louis' done it": Sweet, *Miss Mary Cassatt*, p. 9.
17: "The civilization of the world:" *Philadelphia, A 300-Year History*, p. 336.
18: "He suffered very severely": Hale, *Mary Cassatt*, p. 20.
20: "river of movement": Pool, *Impressionism*, p. 26.
20: "Grey is the enemy": *The Impressionists by Themselves*, p. 9.
21: "the Cad": *Cassatt and Her Circle*, p. 34.
22: "Picture it—think of it": *Cassatt and Her Circle*, p. 34.
22: "good city of P.": *Cassatt and Her Circle*, p. 32.
23: "abolished before the war": *Cassatt and Her Circle*, p. 26.
25: "one does not need": Roudebush, *Cassatt*, p. 7.
25: "born into the world": *Cassatt and Her Circle*, p. 238.

Chapter Three: Finding the Way
26: "the brightest, airiest, and most beautiful": Friedrich, *Olympia*, p. 138.
26: "talking and amusing ourselves": *Cassatt and Her Circle*, p. 56.
29: "ugly, enormous feet": Friedrich, *Olympia*, p. 241.
30: "Insults rain down on me": Courthion, *Impressionism*, p. 73.
30: "There is only one true": Friedrich, *Olympia*, p. 11.
31: "The French school is going": Mathews, *Mary Cassatt*, p. 14.
31: "little, out of the way": Mathews, *Mary Cassatt*, p. 14.
31: "Everything [was] in the most": Mathews, *Mary Cassatt*, p. 14.
32: "getting fat": *Cassatt and Her Circle*, p. 44.
32: "Our little models tease": *Cassatt and Her Circle*, p. 42.
32: "vigor of treatment": *Cassatt and Her Circle*, p. 57.
32: "unmistakeable talent": *Cassatt and Her Circle*, p. 57.
33: "I am constantly dreaming": *Cassatt and Her Circle*, p. 59.
33: "dirt and fleas": *Cassatt and Her Circle*, p. 62.
33: "I believe that we unhappy": Friedrich, *Olympia*, p. 192.

Chapter Four: Old Masters and a New Art
34: "I never dreamed of a catastrophe": Friedrich, *Olympia*, p. 196.
35: "I have given up my studio": *Cassatt and Her Circle*, p. 75.

35: "My eyes water to see": *Cassatt and Her Circle*, p. 77.
36: "Patience is my motto": *Cassatt and Her Circle*, p. 70.
36: "My Dear Little Wife": Sweet, *Miss Mary Cassatt*, p. 24.
37: "I am wild to be off": *Cassatt and Her Circle*, p. 76.
37: "old palazzo [palace] with an": *Cassatt and Her Circle*, p. 84.
37: "innumerable varieties of maccaroni": *Cassatt and Her Circle*, p. 84.
37: "Parma grows upon us": *Cassatt and Her Circle*, p. 88.
38: "that angel": *Cassatt and Her Circle*, p. 92.
38: "For eight months I went": Carson, *Mary Cassatt*, p. 8.
38: "My copy is nearly done": *Cassatt and Her Circle*, p. 99.
40: "All Parma is talking": *Cassatt and Her Circle*, p. 95.
40: "I shine a little": *Cassatt and Her Circle*, p. 95.
41: "Although I think now": *Cassatt and Her Circle*, p. 103.
41: "Velázquez oh! my": *Cassatt and Her Circle*, p. 103.
41: "The men and women have": Mathews, *Mary Cassatt*, p. 26.
41: "like a miserable little 'critter'": *Cassatt and Her Circle*, p. 108.
42: "I want you to know her": Sweet, *Miss Mary Cassatt*, p. 20.
42: "Mary is in high spirits": Roudebush, *Cassatt*, p. 7.
42: "overflowing river": Herbert, *Impressionism*, p. 14.
43: "porcelains, perfumery, bronzes": Herbert, *Impressionism*, p. 14.
43: "Oh how good it is": Mathews, *Mary Cassatt*, p. 29.
44: "I by no means agree": *Cassatt and Her Circle*, p. 117.
44: "very touchy and selfish": *Cassatt and Her Circle*, p. 129.
45: "When I came to live": Mathews, *Mary Cassatt*, p. 30.
45: "too original a style": Effeny, *Cassatt*, p. 14.
46: "Miss Cassatt . . . explained Courbet": Hale, *Mary Cassatt*, p. 105.
47: "How well I remember": Mathews, *Mary Cassatt*, p. 33.

Chapter Five: "There Is Someone Who Feels as I Do"

50: "It's true. There is someone": Sweet, *Miss Mary Cassatt*, p. 31.
50: "If a person is a laughing type": Hüttinger, *Degas*, p. 50.
50: "no worse and no better": Havemeyer, *Sixteen to Sixty*, p. 246.
51: "Life [in Paris] is rich": Hüttinger, *Degas*, p. 41.
51: "I would show the Paris": *The Impressionists by Themselves*, p. 15.
51: "There isn't a person": *The Impressionists by Themselves*, p. 219.
51: "bring out [the] hidden": *The Impressionists by Themselves*, p. 219.
52: "devouring": *The Impressionists by Themselves*, p. 81.
53: "of a monkey who might": Friedrich, *Olympia*, p. 258.
53: "A preliminary drawing for": *The Impressionists by Themselves*, p. 13.
54: "Don't proceed according to": Friedrich, *Olympia*, p. 247.
54: "frightening spectacle": Friedrich, *Olympia*, p. 259.
55: "Try to make M. Pissarro": Friedrich, *Olympia*, p. 259.
55: "In a new age": *Techniques of the Great Masters of Art*, p. 104.
56: "Without him we wouldn't have": *The Impressionists by Themselves*, p. 91.

56: "Art is a matter of": *The Impressionists by Themselves*, p. 93.
56: "Not a penny left": *The Impressionists by Themselves*, p. 92
57: "I accepted with joy": *The Impressionists by Themselves*, p. 85.
58: "She makes pictures": Hale, *Mary Cassatt*, p. 70.
59: "If you were not a genius": Hale, *Mary Cassatt*, p. 71.
59: "Oh, I am independent": Roudebush, *Cassatt*, p. 16.
59: "he finds the movement difficult": Sweet, *Miss Mary Cassatt*, p. 68.
60: "this distinguished person whose": *Cassatt and Her Circle*, p. 148.
61: "Since M. Degas had thought": *The Impressionists by Themselves*, p. 105.
61: "I cannot stop putting": *The Impressionists by Themselves*, p. 106.
61: "Beauty is a mystery": Hale, *Mary Cassatt*, p. 98.
62: "If one wants to be": *The Impressionists by Themselves*, p. 22.
62: "a painter has no private": Carson, *Mary Cassatt*, p. 33.
62: "often weep over": *The Impressionists by Themselves*, p. 106.
62: "My mistake was in not": Hale, *Mary Cassatt*, p. 289.

Chapter Six: Mary Cassatt, Impressionist

63: "Paris is a wonder": Hale, *Mary Cassatt*, p. 79.
64: "We would have liked": Sweet, *Miss Mary Cassatt*, p. 34.
64: "thousand and one . . . delights": Sweet, *Miss Mary Cassatt*, p. 34.
64: "blaze of glory": Hale, *Mary Cassatt*, p. 79.
65: "Gard writes very meagre": Hale, *Mary Cassatt*, p. 80.
65: "Yesterday I received": Hale, *Mary Cassatt*, p. 76.
66: "Mame is working away": Sweet, *Miss Mary Cassatt*, p. 36.
68: "We cannot in fact understand the": *Cassatt and Her Circle*, p. 135.
68: "perhaps the only artists who": Sweet, *Miss Mary Cassatt*, p. 43.
68: "There is nothing more graciously": Effeny, *Cassatt*, p. 17.
69: "She is now known": *Cassatt and Her Circle*, p. 144.
69: "I thank you very much": *Cassatt and Her Circle*, p. 137.
69: "We [French Impressionists] expect": *Cassatt and Her Circle*, p. 137.
70: "I always have a hope": *Cassatt and Her Circle*, p. 137.
70: "It is pleasant to see": Effeny, *Cassatt*, p. 56.
71: "No time to lose": *The Impressionists by Themselves*, p. 111.
71: "Mlle Cassatt is trying": *The Impressionists by Themselves*, p. 112.
72: "Impossible for me": *The Impressionists by Themselves*, p. 112.
72: "Degas is never ready": *Cassatt and Her Circle*, p. 151.
74: "teased his poor Aunt": *Cassatt and Her Circle*, p. 187.
74: "She could hardly sell": Mathews, *Mary Cassatt*, p. 52.
75: "It makes me wish": Lindsay, *Mary Cassatt and Philadelphia*, p. 46.
76: "I don't like to buy": Hale, *Mary Cassatt*, p. 107.
77: "When you get these": *Cassatt and Her Circle*, p. 161.
77: "The sitting business is": Lindsay, *Mary Cassatt and Philadelphia*, p. 61.
77: "I cannot abide Mary": Sweet, *Miss Mary Cassatt*, p. 56.
78: "to draw very carefully": Sweet, *Miss Mary Cassatt*, p. 59.

78: "What [Mary] did in the": Hale, *Mary Cassatt*, p. 103.
79: "This is family life": Hale, *Mary Cassatt*, p. 104.
79: "happy contentment, the quiet": Hale, *Mary Cassatt*, p. 104.
79: "an artist who owes nothing": Hale, *Mary Cassatt*, p. 103.
79: "Too much pudding": *Cassatt and Her Circle*, p. 160.

Chapter Seven: Family Cares

80: "It was on Tuesday": Carson, *Mary Cassatt*, p. 43.
80: "Mother must not be": Carson, *Mary Cassatt*, p. 43.
80: "Give my love to all": Carson, *Mary Cassatt*, p. 43.
80: "Lydia says [Mary] has": Carson, *Mary Cassatt*, p. 44.
81: "Mary seems to be": Carson, *Mary Cassatt*, p. 44.
82: "[Mary] is very lonesome": Carson, *Mary Cassatt*, p. 44.
82: "had to put up with": Sweet, *Miss Mary Cassatt*, p. 77.
82: "I hope [Eddie] won't": *Cassatt and Her Circle*, p. 165.
83: "looking like millers": Sweet, *Miss Mary Cassatt*, p. 76.
83: "Aunt Mary is going to": Sweet, *Miss Mary Cassatt*, p. 78.
83: "Poor child it has been": *Cassatt and Her Circle*, p. 171.
84: "Streams of gold are": *The Impressionists by Themselves*, p. 86.
84: "There are scarcely 15": *The Impressionists by Themselves*, p. 173.
84: "The painting of an unknown": *The Impressionists by Themselves*, p. 173.
84: "Do I care a jot": *The Impressionists by Themselves*, p. 282.
85: "This man has gone sour": Roudebush, *Cassatt*, p. 39.
86: "most lovely old Japanese": *Cassatt and Her Circle*, p. 173.
86: "They are not very artistic": *Cassatt and Her Circle*, p. 174.
88: "I felt I never": Carson, *Mary Cassatt*, p. 59.
88: "distinction itself": *Cassatt and Her Circle*, p. 174.
88: "Study lines, young man": Hüttinger, *Degas*, p. 20.
88: "The dancer is for me": Hüttinger, *Degas*, p. 83.
88: "I'm leaving. All these": *The Impressionists by Themselves*, p. 102.
89: "It has qualities of art": Carson, *Mary Cassatt*, p. 149.
89: "My poor painting is": *Cassatt and Her Circle*, p. 177.
90: "[Father] really cannot be": *Cassatt and Her Circle*, p. 176.
90: "Father went on like": Sweet, *Miss Mary Cassatt*, p. 90.
91: "seize a moment from": *Cassatt and Her Circle*, p. 186.
91: "I am at work": *Cassatt and Her Circle*, p. 195.
91: "He is much delighted": *Cassatt and Her Circle*, p. 195.
92: "Degas doesn't care": *The Impressionists by Themselves*, p. 180.
92: "when you don't have to wonder": *The Impressionists by Themselves*, p. 180.
93: "Needless to say they": *Cassatt and Her Circle*, p. 198.
93: "the totally different future": *The Impressionists by Themselves*, p. 182.
95: "What drawing! What style!": Mathews, *Mary Cassatt*, p. 66.
96: "interesting movement in foreign": Carson, *Mary Cassatt*, p. 67.
96: "Don't think that the Americans": Carson, *Mary Cassatt*, p. 68.

96: "It doesn't think it": Carson, *Mary Cassatt*, p. 66.
97: "rather pleasantly in fact": Sweet, *Miss Mary Cassatt*, p. 111.
97: "He's corrupting all the": *Cassatt and Her Circle*, p. 200.
97: "deprived . . . of her horsewoman's": Sweet, *Miss Mary Cassatt*, p. 112.

Chapter Eight: Japanese Prints and a Chicago Mural
101: "marvellous Impressionist[s]": *The Impressionists by Themselves*, p. 219.
101: "You couldn't dream of anything": Effeny, *Cassatt*, p. 29.
102: "There are two ways": Hale, *Mary Cassatt*, p. 151.
102: "In drypoint you are": Sweet, *Miss Mary Cassatt*, p. 117.
103: "rare and exquisite": Sweet, *Miss Mary Cassatt*, p. 119.
103: "adorable blues, fresh rose": Sweet, *Miss Mary Cassatt*, p. 119.
104: "ugly, heavy, lusterless": Hale, *Mary Cassatt*, p. 153.
104: "I am not willing": Roudebush, *Cassatt*, p. 22.
105: "I am very anxious": *Cassatt and Her Circle*, p. 221.
105: "intent on fame and money": *Cassatt and Her Circle*, p. 222.
105: "I am very glad": *Cassatt and Her Circle*, p. 228.
107: "I am very much depressed": *Cassatt and Her Circle*, p. 227.
107: "At first I was horrified": Effeny, *Cassatt*, p. 32.
108: "as bright, as gay, as amusing": Effeny, *Cassatt*, p. 33.
108: "I am afraid my": *Cassatt and Her Circle*, p. 235.
108: "If he happens to be": Effeny, *Cassatt*, p. 33.
108: "I hardly think women": Sweet, *Miss Mary Cassatt*, p. 129.
108: "Contract received, conditions impossible": *Cassatt and Her Circle*, p. 231.
109: "certainly Chicago seems to": *Cassatt and Her Circle*, p. 243.
110: "Men, I have no doubt": Effeny, *Cassatt*, p. 34.
110: "when it is dragged up": *Cassatt and Her Circle*, p. 238.
111: "After all give me France": *Cassatt and Her Circle*, p. 254.
111: "I suppose it is Mrs. Palmer's": *Cassatt and Her Circle*, p. 254.
112: "Everyone has their criterion": Mathews, *Mary Cassatt*, p. 94.
113: "I do not want to sell": Hale, *Mary Cassatt*, p. 167.
113: "skill that reminds us": Carson, *Mary Cassatt*, p. 101.
113: "all the qualities of": Carson, *Mary Cassatt*, p. 99.
114: "I ask myself when": *Cassatt and Her Circle*, p. 260.
115: "I hope I am now": Carson, *Mary Cassatt*, p. 106.
116: "there is nothing like": Carson, *Mary Cassatt*, p. 106.
116: "I often nurse [Mother]": *Cassatt and Her Circle*, p. 262.
116: "After all a woman": *The Impressionists by Themselves*, p. 269.
117: "It is essential to": *The Impressionists by Themselves*, p. 212.
118: "I am broke, completely broke": *The Impressionists by Themselves*, p. 275.
119: "I hope Miss Cassatt will": *Cassatt and Her Circle*, p. 220
119: "Ah! Sight! Sight!": *The Impressionists by Themselves*, p. 215.
120: "France's honor was at stake": Hale, *Mary Cassatt*, p. 173.
120: "the ferocious anti-Semite": Carson, *Mary Cassatt*, p. 104.

121: "Women should be *someone*": *Cassatt and Her Circle*, p. 254.
121: "great trouble": *Cassatt and Her Circle*, p. 211.
121: "How we try for happiness": Roudebush, *Cassatt*, p. 53.

Chapter Nine: "I Am American"
122: "I am American": Roudebush, *Cassatt*, p. 5.
122: "She is one of the brilliant": Lindsay, *Mary Cassatt and Philadelphia*, p. 9.
122: "Mary Cassatt, sister of": Roudebush, *Cassatt*, p. 75.
124: "The state the pictures": Sweet, *Miss Mary Cassatt*, p. 151.
124: "admire good work": Sweet, *Miss Mary Cassatt*, p. 151.
125: "fairy godmother": Effeny, *Cassatt*, p. 14.
125: "Miss Cassatt had the 'flair'": Havemeyer, *Sixteen to Sixty*, p. 84.
126: "brilliant with life": Havemeyer, *Sixteen to Sixty*, p. 216.
127: "I am American": Roudebush, *Cassatt*, p. 5.
127: "It has been one of": Effeny, *Cassatt*, p. 35.
127: "She was the most devoted": Bullard, *Mary Cassatt, Oils and Pastels*, p. 18.
127: "I work, & that is the whole": Mathews, *Mary Cassatt*, p. 129.
128: "one of the foremost pastellists": Carson, *Mary Cassatt*, p. 120.
129: "I was one of the original": Carson, *Mary Cassatt*, p. 132.
130: "Why should my judgement": Sweet, *Miss Mary Cassatt*, p. 166.
130: "in art what we want": Mathews, *Mary Cassatt*, p. 131.
131: "in these warm still": Carson, *Mary Cassatt*, p. 135.
131: "The whole beauty of the place": Bullard, *Mary Cassatt, Oils and Pastels*, p. 58.
132: "Here, Taudy, you can have": Sweet, *Miss Mary Cassatt*, p. 212.
135: "a fiery and peppery lady": Sweet, *Miss Mary Cassatt*, p. 170.
135: "No Frenchman of any": Mathews, *Mary Cassatt*, p. 136.
136: "I feel as if a force": Carson, *Mary Cassatt*, p. 138.
136: "I too mourn a friend": Hale, *Mary Cassatt*, p. 207.
137: "Isn't it splendid to": *Cassatt and Her Circle*, p. 303.
137: "see through the mysterious": Hale, *Mary Cassatt*, p. 186.
137: "life is going on": Sweet, *Miss Mary Cassatt*, p. 180.
138: "there is no better investment": Sweet, *Miss Mary Cassatt*, p. 162.
138: "Miss Cassatt was the only": Hale, *Mary Cassatt*, p. 216.
140: "It seems so odd": *Cassatt and Her Circle*, p. 304.
141: "I am pining to": Hale, *Mary Cassatt*, p. 231.
141: "I feel so utterly": Hale, *Mary Cassatt*, p. 233.
141: "Now I am the only one": Sweet, *Miss Mary Cassatt*, p. 189.
141: "There is no use": Sweet, *Miss Mary Cassatt*, p. 189.
142: "I have worked so hard": *Cassatt and Her Circle*, p. 313.
142: "She has had a long illness": Hale, *Mary Cassatt*, p. 254.

Chapter Ten: War and Roses
146: "The world is mad just now": Sweet, *Miss Mary Cassatt*, p. 191.

147: "My dear dear Theodate": *Cassatt and Her Circle*, p. 323.
147: "In this sea of misery": Sweet, *Miss Mary Cassatt*, p. 192.
147: "I never felt so isolated": *Cassatt and Her Circle*, p. 323.
149: "The sight of that picture": Mathews, *Mary Cassatt*, p. 149.
150: "A man should marry": Hale, *Mary Cassatt*, p. 247.
150: "Of course you have seen": Roudebush, *Cassatt*, p. 80.
151: "It is the impossibility": Carson, *Mary Cassatt*, p. 168.
152: "I have no respect": Sweet, *Miss Mary Cassatt*, p. 201.
152: "A woman artist must be": Hale, *Mary Cassatt*, p. 150.
153: "One continues to the last day": *The Impressionists by Themselves*, p. 215.
154: "I have not done": *Cassatt and Her Circle*, p. 333.

Selected Bibliography

Boyle, Richard J. *American Impressionism.* Boston: Little, Brown, 1990.

Brettell, Richard R. *French. Salon Artists, 1800–1900.* New York: Art Institute of Chicago and Harry N. Abrams, 1987.

Bullard, John E. *Mary Cassatt, Oils and Pastels.* New York: Watson-Guptil, 1972.

Carson, Julia M. H. *Mary Cassatt.* New York: David McKay, 1966.

Cassatt and Her Circle: Selected Letters. Edited by Nancy Mowll Mathews. New York: Abbeville Press, 1984.

Collins, Amy Fine. *American Impressionism.* New York: Gallery Books, 1990.

Courthion, Pierre. *Impressionism.* New York: Harry N. Abrams, 1977.

Davis, Patricia. *End of the Line: Alexander J. Cassatt and the Pennsylvania Railroad.* New York: Neale Watson Academic Publications, 1978.

Effeny, Alison. *Cassatt: The Masterworks.* New York: Portland House, 1991.

Friedrich, Otto. *Olympia.* New York: HarperCollins, 1992.

Gerdts, William H. *American Impressionism.* New York: Artabras, 1984.

Getlein, Frank. *Mary Cassatt: Paintings and Prints.* New York: Abbeville Press, 1980.

Hale, Nancy. *Mary Cassatt.* Garden City, NY: Doubleday, 1975.

Havemeyer, Louisine W. *Sixteen to Sixty: Memoirs of a Collector.* New York: Metropolitan Museum of Art, 1961.

Herbert, Robert L. *Impressionism.* New Haven: Yale University Press, 1988.

Horwitz, Sylvia L. *Toulouse-Lautrec: His World*. New York: Harper and Row, 1973.

Hüttinger, Edward. *Degas*. New York: Crown, 1977.

The Impressionists by Themselves. Edited by Michael Howard. New York: Smithmark, 1991.

Leaders of American Impressionism. Brooklyn Institute of Arts and Sciences Museum. New York: Arno Press, 1974.

Lindsay, Suzanne G. *Mary Cassatt and Philadelphia*. Philadelphia: Philadelphia Museum of Art, 1985.

Mathews, Nancy Mowll. *Mary Cassatt*. New York: Harry N. Abrams, 1987.

Mathews, Nancy Mowll. *Mary Cassatt: The Color Prints*. New York: Harry N. Abrams, 1988.

Myers, Elisabeth. *Mary Cassatt: A Portrait*. Chicago: Reilly and Lee Books, 1971.

Philadelphia: A 300-Year History. Edited by Russell F. Weigley. New York: W. W. Norton, 1982.

Pool, Phoebe. *Impressionism*. London: Thames and Hudson, 1967.

Renoir, Jean. *Renoir, My Father*. Boston: Little, Brown, 1962.

Roudebush, Jay. *Cassatt*. New York: Crown, 1977.

Scheader, Catherine. *Mary Cassatt*. Chicago: Regensterner, 1977.

Ségard, Achille. *Mary Cassatt: Un Peintre des Enfants et des Mères*. Paris: Librairie Paul Ollendorff, 1913.

Sweet, Frederick A. *Miss Mary Cassatt: Impressionist from Pennsylvania*. Norman: University of Oklahoma Press, 1966.

Techniques of the Great Masters of Art. London: Chartwell Books, 1985.

Index

Academy 27, 28, 29, 30, 44, 51, 52
Allegheny City, Pennsylvania 8, 11
aquatint 102, 103
Assumption of the Virgin 126
At the Milliner's 59

The Bath 117, 118
Belle Époque 99, 112, 145
The Boating Party 113
Boston 123, 124
boycotts 29, 85, 92
Boy in the Sailor Suit 111
Bracquemond, Félix 71, 72

The Caress 129
Cassatt, Alexander (Aleck) 8, 12, 14, 17, 18, 35, 36, 42, 63, 64, 65, 69, 70, 72, 73, 75, 76, 77, 78, 80, 81, 82, 86, 89, 90, 91, 93, 95, 97, 107, 116, 123, 136
Cassatt, Eddie 64, 73, 82, 83, 123
Cassatt, Ellen Mary 121, 123, 139, 140, 145, 153
Cassatt, Elsie 73, 123
Cassatt, Eugenia 123, 137, 139, 140, 145
Cassatt, Gardner (Gard) (brother) 8, 14, 18, 63, 65, 82, 91, 93, 96, 111, 121, 123, 139, 141
Cassatt, Gardner Jr. 97, 111, 112, 121, 123
Cassatt, Jennie 82, 139
Cassatt, Joseph 8
Cassatt, Katharine (niece) 65, 73, 123, 135
Cassatt, Katherine (mother) 8, 9, 10, 11, 17, 25, 40, 63, 64, 65, 70, 72, 74, 80, 86, 89, 90, 97, 111, 116, 121, 123
Cassatt, Lois 36, 42, 63, 73, 77, 78, 81, 82, 83, 90, 123, 136
Cassatt, Lydia 8, 14, 17, 63, 64, 65, 66, 68, 73, 75, 80, 81, 85, 121
Cassatt, Robbie (nephew) 73, 74, 78, 123, 145
Cassatt, Robert (father) 8, 9, 10, 11, 12, 16, 18, 20, 21, 25, 35, 36, 40, 63, 64, 65, 66, 69, 75, 77, 80, 82, 90, 91, 93, 97, 106, 107, 121, 123
Cassatt, Robert (Robbie) (brother) 8, 14, 18
Cézanne, Paul 51, 84, 115, 126
Château de Beaufresne 114, 115, 116, 121, 131, 132, 133, 139, 145, 146, 147, 151, 152, 153
chiaroscuro 28, 30
Child in Orange Dress 128
Child with Red Hat 128
Correggio 37, 38, 41
Courbet, Gustave 29, 30, 44, 46, 52, 115, 126
A Cup of Tea 68

The Dancer 151

Degas, Edgar 6, 20, 46, 47, 49, 50, 51, 52, 53, 57, 58, 59, 60, 61, 62, 66, 67, 68, 70, 71, 72, 73, 76, 77, 78, 84, 85, 88, 89, 92, 93, 94, 95, 97, 98, 104, 108, 113, 115, 117, 118, 119, 120, 125, 126, 128, 135, 139, 142, 149, 150, 151, 152, 153
Delacroix, Eugène 19, 20
Domenec, Bishop Michael 36, 38
Dreyfus Affair 119, 120
drypoint 102, 151, 152
Durand-Ruel, Paul 54, 55, 56, 83, 84, 95, 96, 104, 105, 113, 114, 119, 129, 133

Eakins, Thomas 23, 26, 27
École des Beaux-Arts 27, 28, 101
education 9, 14, 17, 136
Eighth Impressionist Exhibit 93, 95
Ellen Mary Cassatt in a White Coat 121
Elsie in a Blue Chair 75
Exposition Universelle 19, 61, 63, 64

Fifth Impressionist Exhibit 68
Fourth Impressionist Exhibit 67, 69
Franco-Prussian War 33, 34, 42, 64, 122

Gauguin, Paul 100
Gérôme, Jean-Léon 27
Girl Arranging Her Hair 94, 95, 151

Haldeman, Eliza 21, 22, 23, 26, 27, 31, 32, 33
Havemeyer, Henry O. 82, 95, 124, 125, 126, 127, 132, 133, 136, 138, 146
Havemeyer, Louisine Elder 45, 46, 47, 50, 59, 76, 77, 82, 95, 107, 120, 121, 124, 125, 126, 127, 132, 133, 136, 138, 141, 142, 146, 147, 148, 150, 151, 152
Hiroshige 101, 103
Huysmans, J. K. 55, 79

Impression: Sunrise 53
Impressionists 53, 54, 55, 56, 57, 58, 60, 61, 66, 67, 69, 73, 76, 77, 81, 83, 84, 85, 86, 88, 89, 91, 92, 93, 94, 95, 96, 98, 100, 101, 103, 118, 124, 128, 135, 137, 138, 154
Independents 52, 53, 68, 89, 118, 124, 129, 135
Ingres, Jean-Auguste-Dominique 19, 20, 28, 88, 138
intaglio 71, 102, 103

Japan 101, 102, 103, 104, 113, 115
Johnston, Alexander 9
Johnston, Colonel James 9

Lady at the Tea Table 85, 88, 149

La Mandoline 32
Lambdin, James 13, 14
La Répétition de Ballet 46, 47
Le Déjeuner sur l'herbe 30
Le Jour et La Nuit 70, 72
The Letter 104
Little Girl in a Blue Armchair 60, 61, 64
Louvre Museum 27, 59, 71
Lydia in a Loge, Wearing a Pearl Necklace 66, 67
Lydia Leaning on Her Arms, Seated in a Loge 73
Lydia Working at a Tapestry Frame 81

Madame Cortier 49
The Majas on the Balcony 126
Manet, Edouard 29, 30, 33, 41, 44, 51, 52, 53, 56, 95, 113, 126
Margot in Blue 132
Marly-le-Roi 73, 74, 78, 79, 81
Mesnil-Théribus 132, 133
Metropolitan Museum of Art 105, 127, 138, 149, 152
Modern Woman 107, 109
Monet, Claude 29, 44, 51, 52, 53, 56, 68, 76, 84, 88, 93, 95, 118, 120, 126, 135
Morisot, Berthe 6, 53, 58, 67, 76, 93, 96, 101, 115
Mother About to Wash Her Sleepy Child 75
Mrs. Cassatt Reading to Her Grandchildren 74, 96

Napoléon III, Louis 16, 19, 26, 33, 34, 42, 43
Neo-Impressionism 94, 100
New York 13, 36, 69, 70, 95, 96, 105, 111, 127, 129, 138, 146, 149, 152

Old Masters 25, 27, 33, 38, 40, 58, 77, 125, 135, 138, 149

Palmer, Bertha 107, 108, 109, 110, 111
Paris Opera House 66, 67, 71
Parma, Italy 36, 37, 38, 40
Pennsylvania Academy of the Fine Arts 21, 22, 23, 27, 69, 71, 129, 130
Pissarro, Camille 6, 51, 53, 54, 55, 56, 68, 71, 76, 77, 85, 92, 93, 94, 96, 101, 103, 104, 115, 118, 119, 120
Pittsburgh, Pennsylvania 8, 10, 11, 36, 38
Pope, Theodate 136, 137, 140, 146, 147
pointillism 94
Primitive Woman 107
printmaking 71, 72, 101, 102, 103, 104, 105, 112, 120, 154

Reading Le Figaro 70, 96
Realist movement 29, 30
Renoir, Pierre-Auguste 6, 44, 50, 52, 53, 56, 66, 76, 84, 93, 96, 113, 118, 135
Riddle, Mrs. Robert Moore 86, 123

Salon 29, 30, 32, 33, 35, 40, 41, 44, 45, 49, 50, 51, 52, 53, 55, 57, 60, 84, 85, 92, 100, 129
Sartain, Emily 35, 36, 37, 38, 40, 41, 43, 44
Second Impressionist Exhibit 54
Ségard, Achille 25, 122
Seurat, Georges 94
Seventh Impressionist Exhibit 85
Simone in a White Bonnet 128
Sisley, Alfred 51, 96
The Sisters 91
Society of American Artists 69, 70
Society of Painters-Printmakers 103
soft-ground etching 102, 103
Stillman, James 138, 139, 142, 143, 148
Summertime 131
Sunday Afternoon on the Island of La Grande Jatte 94
Susan on a Balcony Holding a Dog 94

Third Republic 35, 42
tondos 130
Toulouse-Lautrec, Henri de 100
Tourny, Joseph 49, 50
Two Children at the Seashore 91
Two Women Throwing Flowers During Carnival 40

Utamaro 101, 103

Vallet, Mathilde 90, 132, 133, 142, 143, 146, 151, 153
Velázquez 25, 41
View of Toledo 126
Villa Angeletto 139, 142, 146
Vollard, Ambroise 129, 133, 150

Woman Bathing 104
women's suffrage 136, 139, 148, 149
wood-block printing 101, 102, 115
World's Columbian Exposition 107, 109, 110, 111
World War I 99, 145, 146, 147

Young Mother Sewing 128

Zola, Émile 120